Living Simply in an Anxious World

Robert J. Wicks

Paulist Press
New York/Mahwah, New Jersey

Cover/book design and interior illustrations by Nicholas T. Markell.

Copyright © 1988, 1998 by Robert J. Wicks

Library of Congress Cataloging-in-Publication Data

Wicks, Robert J.
    Living simply in an anxious world / by Robert J. Wicks.
        p.   cm. — (IlluminationBooks)
    Originally published : New York : Paulist Press, ©1988.
    Includes bibliographical references.
    ISBN 0-8091-3767-4 (alk. paper)
    1. Spiritual life—Catholic Church. 2. Psychology and religion.
I. Title. II. Series.
BX2350.2.W525   1998
248.4′82—dc21
                                         97-35334
                                           CIP

Published by Paulist Press
997 Macarthur Boulevard
Mahwah, New Jersey 07430

Printed and bound in the
United States of America

Contents

IlluminationBooks
A Foreword

When this series was launched in 1994, I wrote that Illumination-Books were conceived to "bring to light wonderful ideas, helpful information, and sound spirituality in concise, illustrative, readable, and eminently practical works on topics of current concern."

In keeping with this premise, among the first books were offerings by well-known authors Joyce Rupp *(Little Pieces of Light...Darkness and Personal Growth)* and Basil Pennington *(Lessons from the Monastery That Touch Your Life)*. In addition, there were titles by up-and-coming authors and experts in the fields of spirituality and psychology. These books covered a wide array of topics: joy, controlling stress and anxiety, personal growth, discernment, caring for others, the mystery of the Trinity, celebrating the woman you are, and facing your own desert experiences.

The continued goal of the series is to provide great ideas, helpful steps, and needed inspiration in small volumes. Each of the books offers a new opportunity for the reader to explore possibilities and embrace practicalities that can be employed in everyday life. Thus, among the new and noteworthy themes for readers to discover are these: how to be more receptive to the love in our lives, simple ways to structure a personal day of recollection, a creative approach to enjoy reading sacred scriptures, and spiritual and psychological methods of facing discouragement.

Like the IlluminationBooks before them, forthcoming volumes are meant to be a source of support—without requiring an inordinate amount of time or prior preparation. To this end, each small work stands on its own. The hope is that the information provided not only will be nourishing in itself but also will encourage further exploration in the area.

When we view the world through spiritual eyes, we appreciate that sound knowledge is really useful only when it can set the stage for *metanoia*, the conversion of our hearts. Each of the IlluminationBooks is designed to contribute in some small but significant way to this process. So, it is with a sense of hope and warm wishes that I offer this particular title and the rest of the series to you.

–Robert J. Wicks
General Editor, IlluminationBooks

Chapter One
An Invitation to Perspective

*T*he seeds of joy grow best in a field of peace. Yet, much of the time most of us seem to live with some degree of anxiety or uncertainty. Moreover, our upset may occasionally escalate to the point where deep turmoil and personal doubt arise.

Losing perspective is easy, even when surrounded by interpersonal and material abundance. One minute we may feel well-grounded in the human family and experience the consolation of God; the next we seem to be standing alone at the edge of a psychological peninsula with our back toward the mainland. At that moment, although we may have a vague understanding that (in Julian of Norwich's words) "all will be well," our hearts still believe we are really on an emotional island lost at sea.

How is it possible for us to lose our way so quickly? Maybe the answer lies partially in our inability to maintain perspective through tenacious trust and hope in a God that must always be as *real* as the problems we face each day.

God really has only one expectation of us: *to love*. But since we find this (in our lack of hope, trust, and patience) too difficult to accept, we try to break down this call and replace it with our own human-fashioned ones. So, the expectation to love is erased from our hearts, and the expectations to do, achieve, gain acceptance, control, be secure, or look good are put in our heads instead. There they remain as lies to preoccupy, confuse, and trouble us. There the purpose they serve is to help us avoid facing the challenge of the real, the deep, the ultimate, the first and final question of life. However, despite this "advantage" or secondary gain, they still leave us lost until eventually we are willing in humility to embrace the only God-given question we must answer: *"How can I love?"*

Obviously we must act; James's controversial epistle faces us with this reality. It is equally valid (as shall be seen later) that action in itself is revelatory. However, even given this, we do need to be quiet enough in our hearts and daily schedule so we can be responsive to what God is telling us. As is emphasized throughout Jeremiah: if they listen to me, I will be their God and they will be my people.

How well we listen will determine our response... or lack of it! Really listening, so that our outlook can be transformed, requires an openness that is certain to meet with resistance on both a psychological and a spiritual level. Knowing this can be helpful in our quest to greet grace—whether that grace be the source of deep consolation or confrontation, whereas not to expect such conscious and unconscious blocks to the search for the unfolding of the truth about ourselves and God would be dangerously naive.

The psychological:
An invitation to perspective

Changes in one's attitude and approach to life are areas in which psychotherapists have had a long-standing interest. Because of this, they are aware of the resistance to change that people have—even when there is an expressed conscious desire to progress. One way of dealing with such resistance, bad habits, or unwanted yet seemingly ingrained negative patterns is to address one or all of the following: *cognition* (styles of thinking, perceiving, and understanding), *imagery, behavior,* and *affect* (feelings, mood, or emotions).

For instance, when a depressed person comes in for treatment, the problems during the course of counseling or therapy are usually dealt with in these areas. In the past when psychotherapy was primarily psychoanalytically-oriented, there was a strong emphasis on *affect.* This was understandable since most people's presenting complaints have to do with a distortion in mood (e.g., depression, anxiety, etc.); people come in because they don't *feel* well emotionally. The goal was to get the patients to relive early relationships in the room. By transferring onto the therapist the feelings they had toward significant figures present during the early formative years, the hope was that a new corrective experience might occur. The problem with this therapeutic approach was that it was essentially long term. Many patients not only could not afford the time and money, but such an extensive effort was sometimes not necessary to produce the desired results. (Focusing primarily on affect or feelings wasn't successful in many cases.)

Today, most therapists carefully draw from a number of therapeutic schools of thought. They are referred to as "*systematic* eclectic therapists." (I emphasize "systematic" because I once heard Dr. Arnold Lazarus refer to eclecticism as "having both feet firmly planted...in mid-air!") Thus, they not only focus on a persons's feelings but also employ an array of other approaches that are outgrowths of a broad therapeutic model.

So, in the case of depression, the therapist or counselor might actually focus on cognition, imagery, and behavior as well as being concerned about the person's feelings. The following is a brief explanation of this.

Cognition: Person is assisted in recognizing negative thinking, seeking the link between it and experiencing depression, and is taught how to correct for this thinking as a way of dealing ultimately with a negative belief system.

Imagery: Person is given exercises in positive imagery as a means of correcting the inordinate negative images that the person frequently has and erroneously believes.

Behavior: Person is helped to develop a strategy to get out of bed and move about, since activity and depression do not coexist well together.

Affect: Person is encouraged to express negative emotion (i.e., anger) so it is not directed against the self in a destructive fashion.

In this four-pronged approach, the person is able to reeducate himself/herself so that, rather than perceiving, imaging, behaving, and feeling negatively, a more realistically balanced and positive way takes greater and greater hold.

The spiritual:
An invitation to simplicity and single-mindedness

Using the above model, similar approaches can be used to encourage our openness to God's grace so our sense of spirituality can mature and remain vital and alive. For instance, with *faith,* appreciating our cognitive style (the way we think and believe) becomes an opportunity to *listen* to God. With *hope,* imaging ourselves and the world anew becomes an invitation to *see* God in different ways. With *love,* our behavior becomes an example of true *service* to God. And, with *prayer,* our affect (emotion) becomes a chance to *experience* God as never before. So, with *grace,* our psychological abilities to attain perspective can become transformed into a spirituality that seeks *simplicity* and *single-mindedness.* To understand the import of this and to set the stage for the remainder of the book, let's now briefly look at the relationship between the psychological and the spiritual in these four areas (*cognition/listening, imagery/seeing, behavior/service, affect/experiencing*).

Cognition/listening to God

The power of perception is amazing. What is a challenging opportunity for one is an unbearable problem for another. We are generally not aware of how much power we really have. When upset, the almost automatic assumption is that if only something or someone in the environment would change, I'd feel better. The thought almost never occurs that the power may be in our own hands to perceive the situation in a way that can be the most beneficial. Consequently, much energy is wasted on lamenting or trying to control others or the situation. Nowhere is this more evident than in interpersonal relations.

Anthony de Mello illustrates this beautifully with rich imagery that is easy to retain when we are in difficulty. "To a disciple who was forever complaining about others, the Master said, "'If it is peace you want, seek to change yourself, not other people. *It is easier to protect your feet with slippers than to carpet the whole of the earth.'*" (Italics supplied.)[1]

The same can be said of personal failure. "When we as committed Christians lose our perspective with regard to failure, we ignore the need for self-acceptance as a prelude to personal growth. Instead of forgiveness leading to an openness which will in turn translate into self-understanding, it leads to self-punishment. In such a case as this, we believe that we are seeking forgiveness by crucifying ourselves for our weaknesses. As we do this, the energy formerly reserved for knowledge gets destructively channeled off into changing the process of self-understanding into one of self-condemnation. Nothing positive is accomplished when this happens."[2]

The point being made then is: *How* we perceive something is much more important than *what* we perceive. If we have *faith*, real discernment becomes possible. When we reflect on something, the way we listen to our thoughts and beliefs will be an opportunity to listen to God's voice rather than our own fragile ego trying unnecessarily to protect or crucify itself.

Even pain, rather than being only troubling, can also be quite revelatory. Albert Nolan, the Dominican priest who is known for his work in South Africa, once said: "There is nothing to replace the immediate contact with pain and hunger—seeing people in the cold and rain after their houses have been bulldozed, or experiencing the intolerable smell in a slum, or seeing what children look like when they are suffering from malnutrition."[3] In saying this, his message was not one of despair and defeatism, it was one of faith. To a faith-full person, such an experience would certainly hurt, but, more than that, it would lead to compassion. Faith gives us the opportunity to listen for the call of Christ in pain just as we listen to his support and encouragement during times of joy. With such faith, no matter what the circumstances, the step toward hope is a real and natural one.

Imagery/seeing God

With hope that is based solely on a faith in the resurrection of Christ, the way we see the world becomes radically altered. In David Steindl-Rast's words, "The eyes of hope are grateful eyes. Before our eyes learned to look gratefully at the world, we expected to find beauty in good-looking things. But grateful eyes expect the surprise of finding beauty in *all* things."[4]

Our imagery is never the same once we have hope. The way we view ourselves and the world becomes an opportunity to see "all things new." The way we view ourselves is transformed in that even in failure—maybe *especially* in failure—we seek to learn about the Christ within us. This does not take away the pain of loss and defeat but it removes us from being tied to our accomplishments, the reactions of others, and the images we project. Once again, Steindl-Rast clearly makes this differentiation for us. "A person of hope will have a whole array of lively hopes. But those hopes do not tell us much. The showdown comes when all of the hopes get shattered. Then, a person of hopes will get shattered with them. A person of hope, however, will be growing a new crop of hopes a soon as the storm is over."[5]

The image we have of others also becomes something quite surprising when we have Christian hope. No longer do we have unrealistic expectations. Instead, we have *low expectations and high hopes.* By that I mean our outlook toward, and actions with, others are no longer dependent upon their response. As a matter of fact we act sometimes almost in spite of what people say and do. And we see possibilities where there are seemingly none. The following story by Mother Teresa of Calcutta illustrates this clearly:

> We have a place in Australia. (As you know, many of the aborigines live there in very bad conditions!)
>
> When we went around in that place, we found an old man in a most terrible condition.
>
> I went in there and tried to talk to him and then I said to him, "Kindly allow me to clean your place and clean your bed and so on." He answered, "I'm all right!"

I said to him, "You will be more all right if I clean your place."

In the end he allowed me to do it and when I was in his room (I call it a room, but it was not really a room!) I noticed that he had a lamp, a very beautiful lamp but covered with dirt and dust. I said to him, "Do you not light the lamp?" And he said, "For whom? Nobody comes here. I never see anybody. Nobody comes to me. I don't need to light the lamp."

Then I asked him, "If the sisters come to you, will you light the lamp for them?" He answered, "Yes, I'll do it!"

So the sisters started going to him in the evening and he used to light the lamp.

Afterward (he lived for more than two years), he sent word to me through the sisters and said, "Tell my friend, the light she lit in my life is still burning!"[6]

Behavior/service to God

If our reflective periods are steeped in faith and our imagery is marked by hope, then our behavior can be inspired by love so that what we do is able to be true service to God. The opportunities are certainly there. As Martin Buber once said, "All real living is meeting."

Love breaks through all preconceptions we have about what service to others and God actually is. Many of us have a sense of the dramatic and feel that real service can only be appreciated under such circumstances. The truth is obviously that real service need not always be obvious.

An image of a stained glass window might help bring this point across. Normally, we appreciate stained glass (as we appreciate our service to God) when it is bright and obvious. Yet, there are many other times when the glass presents us with its beauty and character in a less startling way. During different times of day...and times of year, during times of celebration...and times of sorrow, during times of visible community...and times of solitude, the windows allow the light to come through in different shades and intensities of color.

We are like this stained glass, if only we—in a Spirit of love—appreciate this fact. As on a gray rainy day when the light and color coming through the glass is muted in its presence to us, we are similarly present to people in a special way when we sit quietly and actively listen to them and their stories. Just as when night falls, and we sit in a quiet church feeling the leaden presence of the tall massive stained glass windows, yet can't see their colorful presence in front of us, people also take heart from knowing in our physical absence that we are still there for them. (We are thinking about, and praying for, them.)

In other words, with love we begin to see our entire day, and the whole array of interactions that are possible, as *opportunity*. No longer is service to God compartmentalized, nor need it be sharply visible. Instead, it is all service, all love, all a time for a form of community life. Yet, for this to be possible, we must become alert to the love hidden in our hearts and in our day through the presence of constant *prayer*.

Affect/experiencing God

Have you noticed what happens when we move away from the original source of our motivation for service to God? What occurs when we get involved, and almost enamored, with our daily schedule, monthly goals, and the year's planning? Such numerous objectives and good things to accomplish (our apostolate) are like a fire. We are by it with its light and warmth and in our commitment to keep it roaring, we go to gather wood. After a good deal of time, we come back dirty, tired, splintered, and overburdened, only to find the embers barely alive or the fire out, the hearth cold. Our work, even if it was deemed God's work (i.e., supporting our family or community, ministry, efforts for the poor) now seems dead. We feel skeptical, defeated, bored, tired, or under great stress or depression. We wonder where the excitement and fulfillment has gone. We feel God has abandoned us and we even question the previous feelings we have had with respect to our spiritual relationship. What has happened? The absence of true prayer, in most cases, is the answer.

Prayer allows us to experience God as never before. It opens our eyes to the world in a special way. It cuts away the layers of secularism which have kept true meaning away from our hearts. Quite simply: prayer surprises us!

In a local abbey, celebration of the Eucharist was going on. The celebrant was an Indian Norbertine priest. As is the custom in his land, just prior to remembering Christ with the words, "This is my Body....This is my Blood," he removed his shoes as a sign of respect. He was acknowledging what was about to happen; he was acknowledging that he would soon be in the presence of God in a unique way. He knew that shortly he would be on holy ground. Through his actions he wanted to confirm this fact both to himself and to those present.

People reacted to this with surprise. The actions of a person from another culture broke through the crust of their own culture and opened their eyes. For some, it was perhaps the first time they recognized the import of the moment of consecration. In a broader sense this is what true prayer always does. It allows us to be exposed to the culture of Christ—a culture that can form us anew so we don't have to remain sculpted according to how the world at large has slowly fashioned us. This then allows us to experience the world and act in it in a very different way, for *how* we pray significantly changes how we live. In the words of James Fenhagen, "People live cautiously because they pray cautiously."[7]

Perspective/simplicity and single-mindedness

The concept is simple: with *grace*, the invitation to perspective can become transformed into a spirituality that seeks simplicity and single-mindedness. Yet, as can be surmised from the points made thus far, it may be simple but it isn't necessarily easy!

Many times, we do give attention in faith to what we are thinking and believing. We do seek to guide our imagery with hope. We are concerned about where love is motivating our behavior. And we are involved radically in prayer so as to open up our understanding of what we are feeling and experiencing. Yet, despite these efforts, both perspective and simplicity still seem to elude us; we may feel that *nothing* seems to be happening! We may ask, "Where is God in my life?"

This question and the situation to which it refers reminds me of the reflections of a character in Peter Schaefer's movie *Amadeus*. In the beginning of the movie, the action centered around a rivalry between Mozart and Signore Salieri, the court composer. In one of the scenes, Mozart has been asked to compose something special for the court. Before he begins to play it, Salieri, who is jealous, looks over Mozart's shoulder at the music and reflects to himself as follows: "On the page it looked nothing. The beginning simple, almost comic. Just a pulse. Bassoons. Bassett horns. Like a rusty squeezebox. And then suddenly high above it an oboe. A single note hanging there unwavering until a clarinet took it over and sweetened it into a phrase of such delight. This was no composition by a performing monkey. This was a music I'd never heard. Filled with such longing, such unfulfillable longing. It seemed to me that I was hearing the voice of God."[8]

This indeed is what we may experience if we are open to the epiphany (the awakening) of God in our own lives. The rhapsody may well be hidden; all we do to gain perspective and position ourselves to receive the grace of simplicity may seem useless. But patience, persistence, and (most of all) mindfulness of our ultimate dependence on God will be rewarded.

On the feast of the Epiphany, many churches celebrate the time in which the Word was shared, beyond the bounds of the Jewish people, with the Gentiles. In a very similar vein, the epiphany we experience here in our search for psychological perspective and spiritual simplicity is another major movement to be noted and celebrated. It, too, is an extension of the Word, in that it marks the movement of God from those parts of our personality that are already integrated into our Christian self to those parts which still remain in the darkness (i.e., those distorted thoughts/beliefs, images, behaviors, and feelings which don't now bring us closer to God).

The epiphanies to come are still many. The process of enlightenment takes a lifetime and sometimes seems to take place in darkness. Yet, it is a movement that is always marked by consolation if we make the effort to hold on, as securely as we can, to love—a love defined as "being in relationship with God."

Maybe then as we attempt to trace God's presence in our beliefs, images, behaviors, and feelings, the *awe* will return to our lives. The appreciation for life in all of its forms will grow again.

A number of years ago, Alan Watts used to tell a story about an eccentric physicist he knew at the University of Chicago. This scientist was so much impressed by the (molecular) instability of the physical world that he used to go around in enormous padded slippers for fear he would fall through the floor.

If only we could begin to develop such a form of "craziness" and sensitivity with respect to God! Ironically, maybe then our minds would become clearer, our images sharper, our behavior less hampered, and our emotions more responsive. Certainly, at the very least, if we took such a radical note of God's constant presence in ourselves, others, and the world at large, we would never be the same. Our hearts would never permit it.

Chapter Two
Listening

*D*iscernment is a spiritual movement in which we try to decide who God is "calling" us to be and what we are being asked to do in specific instances now and for the future. Without grace, without God, there is (by definition) no process of discernment. There are times when all of the careful problem-solving in the world will achieve nothing. We are at an impasse. It is a time of special appreciation of our dependence on God's mercy and guidance. Yet, this point in no way contradicts or alleviates our responsibility to be as clear as possible when we face each day and the major decisions of life.

"In today's complex and duplicitous world, where the Gospel of Christ can become so easily rationalized and domesticated by us as we face an anxious world, all efforts must be made to be open, clear, and face the Truth....Any assistance we can get to help us in this pursuit should be, must be welcomed."[1]

Clarity brings with it great possibilities that are already present in our life but are missed. Or, as de Mello noted in one of his final writings: "Life is like a motor car...(it) can be used to travel to the heights...but most people lie in front of it, allow it to run over them and then blame it for the accident."[2]

To think and believe clearly is to have the power to cut through many of our unnecessary needs to worry, control, complain, be anxious or angry, be depressed, or feel unloved. To maintain an attitude of discernment (i.e., to be really open to the realities about ourselves and the world in which we live) also requires that we face our illusions, delusions, and allusions. To do this, we must be prepared to meet the many inherent defenses that we have built up. And for this we must have an ability to forgive ourselves and allow ourselves to be surprised by a God who is not modeled by ourselves or someone else. Yet, once again, as in the case of perspective as a whole, whereas understanding the process of seeking clarity seems simple and straightforward, effectively undertaking it certainly is not!

Listening with faith

Developing an attitude that cuts through the psychological brush that keeps us from hearing the truth is a worthwhile goal for us to have today. Listening with faith to our thoughts, beliefs, perceptions, and interpretations is not a mere religious gesture; it is downright mental Christian anarchy! As Thomas Merton recognized: "To renounce the pleasure of one's dearest illusions about oneself is to die more effectively than one could ever do by allowing oneself to be killed for a clearly conceived personal ideal....The 'impure' heart of fallen man is not merely a heart subject to carnal passion. 'Purity' and 'impurity' in this context mean something more than chastity. The 'impure' heart is a heart filled with fears, anxieties, conflicts, doubts, ambivalences, hesitations, self-contradictions, hatreds, jealousies, compulsive needs, and passionate attachments. All these and a thousand other 'impurities' darken the inner light of the soul but they are neither its chief impurity nor the cause of its impurities. The inner, basic, metaphysical defilement of fallen man is his profound and illusory conviction that he is a god and the universe is centered upon him."[3]

Christian critical thinking can cut to the core of idolatry and bring new light to discernment which is often confined by a misguided uncritical loyalty to the very traditions and religious imagery we were given many years ago. In addition, we are presently more comfortable with, and uncritical of, our unproductive thoughts and distorted negative beliefs than we imagine. Such a marriage to the status quo is unacceptable and unworkable if there is a desire to listen to God. As James Fenhagen points out: "The process of transformation is not without pain. In becoming open to all that is new, there is the pain of letting go of all that is old. *Sometimes the things that hurt us the most are the hardest to discard.* The promise, however, is that in the struggle—that ongoing, ever-changing struggle for growth—God is always present. Through him we are transformed." (Italics supplied.)[4]

The process of developing our own narrow and limited system of beliefs (in lieu of those liberating ones to which God would have us be open) frequently functions beyond our level of awareness. To quote Merton again: "Without realizing it, we allow our nature to de-sensitize our souls so that we cannot perceive graces which we intuitively foresee may prove to be painful."[5]

The irony of all of this is that much of the pain we experience when confronted with grace need not hurt as much. Our problem is that we have put ourselves in front of a prefabricated "superego-oriented God" (i.e., one who is looking over our shoulders seeing if we have done something wrong), rather than an "ego-oriented one" who is calling us in love to be all that we can be. We need to remember the words from *The Jerusalem Community Rule of Life*: "Even should your heart condemn you, God is greater than your heart."[6]

On the other hand, this does not mean that we should try to fashion God into an "Id-oriented God" either (i.e., one who says "Anything goes!"); sacred scriptures never implied such an image. The problem instead needs to be viewed as one of *humility.* True humility allows us to stand as failures before God and feel the love that allows us to learn from our experiences rather than to be crushed by them. The risk is to let go of the anxiety of failure and the temptation to be our own god and universe; the goal is to be dependent on a God whose love sets us free to understand and truly be all that we were intended to become.

Too often we see failure as devastating. Instead, it is a growth-producing opportunity to learn about how we have allowed our hearts to stray from a recognition of the need for the mercy and grace of God. Moreover, failure frequently awakens us to life in a much more dramatic way than success could ever do.

William Sloane Coffin in his autobiography, *Once to Every Man,* told the story about a period in his life while serving as chaplain at Yale when he was experiencing serious marital problems and was considering resigning.

> To his surprise, Kingman Brewster (Yale's president) refused to accept his resignation. He and Brewster had not been seeing eye to eye on Coffin's controversial activities, and the resignation could have been a convenient way for Brewster to rid himself of his troublesome chaplain. Instead, he invited Coffin to move in with him and his wife.
>
> Still not satisfied that he should not resign, Coffin talked it over with his faculty colleague Richard Sewall. Sewall also advised against resignation and gave him a compelling reason. "Bill," he said, "if you have suffered from anything, it is from an aura of too much success. A little failure in your personal life can only improve your ministry."[7]

Our beautiful talents become distorted when success becomes so paramount in our lives. Our thoughts about our image in the eyes of others distorts both our perception of life and the way we live it. *The "prize" of succeeding in meeting our own and others' expectations is only sought and won at the price of losing our effectiveness as Christians.* If we are truly involved, we are bound to fail a great deal. Since we are human we are also bound to do things for immature reasons some of the time. Such errors are natural and not really important as long as we are willing to be honest with ourselves and learn from them. Once again, this takes humility and the willingness to possibly "lose face" in the eyes of others.

In teasing those in ministry about their almost neurotic concern about what people think about them, their actions and motivations, I try to help them to regain perspective by noting: "Why are you so concerned about what people think? So many people think ill of you already—what's a few more?"

Chuang Tzu, the spiritual ancient Chinese philosopher, poetically presents this point with a somewhat different emphasis:

> When an archer is shooting for nothing
> He has all his skill.
> If he shoots for a brass buckle
> He is already nervous.
> If he shoots for a prize of gold
> He goes blind
> Or sees two targets—
> He is out of his mind!

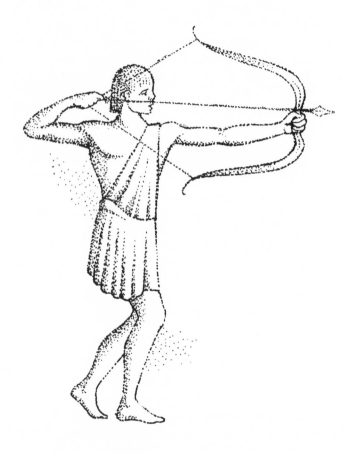

His skill has not changed. But the prize
Divides him. He cares.
He thinks more of winning
Than of shooting—
And the need to win
Drains him of power.[8]

In "shooting" for acceptance and trying to control the outcomes of our daily efforts, we give up the excitement and depth of living and substitute an interest in judging ourselves and others with a yardstick other than love. Such an evaluation unfortunately does not even lead to self-awareness and the appreciation of others. Instead, energy is drained off by self-depreciation and a judgmental attitude as far as others are concerned. This causes a great deal of inner conflict; the joy of living and learning atrophies. It is no wonder the central advice given by the desert father, Abba Joseph, to Abba Poemen was: "If you want to find rest here and hereafter, say on every occasion, 'Who am I?' and do not judge anyone."[9]

To perceive clearly, competition with others must be given up so we can achieve as God would have us. We must trust enough in God so exhibitionism can be given up so we can have the room in our hearts and actions to be enthusiastic. This is not possible though as long as we hold onto the belief that we are only full of love when we do things that win people over or impress them.

Likewise, clarity is not possible if we are unable to be open and flexible enough to hear and embrace the words of love which continually surround us (often in ways possibly foreign to us). A Christian attitude makes the invisible presence of God visible. This is not only with respect to how we give love; but also, in all instances, it must be reflected in our willingness to be humble enough to receive love in ways which are not pre-determined by us.

Too often, without realizing it, we say to ourselves: "This is what love should look like for me. If love is not shown as I think it should, by whom I believe it should, it is not acceptable love to me. I will not accept it!" As a result, while we are remaining bitter because someone "who should" is not treating us as special as we'd like, the smiles and little, quiet, caring attention we are already receiving from others are ignored, dismissed, or passed over. Thus, the needy young man, whose father was angry and disturbed, complains and cries. He chases after similar types of people in his life trying to win over the rejecting authority figure as a magical means of finding the love he didn't receive. In doing this, he misses all of the warm "parental love" that surrounds him in the presence of other affirming family and friends. If people are nice to him, he puts them into one of three categories so the love never reaches him: either "they don't know me" (because if they did they really wouldn't treat me so nicely), they are "just being nice" (but really don't mean it), or "they aren't worth much themselves" (after all, if they like me, how good can they be?).

As William Johnston notes: "The great challenge of the Christian life is to receive love, to open our hearts to the one who knocks, to accept him into the very depth of our being...authentic human love is God's love made incarnate. So accept the love which comes your way. If you think that nobody loves you, this is probably because you are unconsciously warding off love. You are just not taking it in. Accept it with gratitude and you will experience joy."[10]

With our "psychological hands" open we can receive the love that surrounds us from people in places we might not ordinarily look. The smile of a grocery clerk, the wide-eyed stare of a three year old neighbor, and the encouragement of someone who writes or calls us to "just say hello" are all love for us to have. Such love helps us to love ourselves, so learning about ourselves and God's action within us becomes more possible. As we feel we are loved, it is more possible to follow the model of the paraclete in embracing ourselves, our beliefs, thoughts, and perceptions. In the words of the Biblical scholar Donald Senior: "The evangelist gives special emphasis to the role of the Spirit, to use John's unique name, the 'paraclete.' The term 'paraclete' has several nuances of meaning—'comfort,' 'exhort,' 'animate,' 'confront'—each of which captures some glint of the Spirit's action in Christian life."[11]

This very spiritual action must be called for in our discernment of what God is saying to us as we reflect on our own cognitions and try to listen, *really listen,* to how we are interpreting our own actions and motives as well as those of the people with whom we interact. We must model the paraclete then in how we face ourselves. Not to do so is to risk living in the psychological and spiritual darkness of denial.

Deadly denial

With deep faith in a loving God, cutting through the quiet "psychological sin" of denial is necessary since it is so ruinous to our spiritual life and emotional well-being. Yet, ironically, we hear little about denial. Instead, most of the attention is given to overt failures and mistakes. This is a shame since individual and corporate problems that are the worst become so because they are never seen for what they are when they first appear—seeds of personal and societal destruction.

Denial can be quite obvious. When alcoholics or drug addicts sit amidst the shambles of their lives and deny that they have a problem, no one is fooled. When we hear companies that pollute the air and the water claim they did not realize the impact of their actions over the past fifteen years, we doubt the veracity of their statements. However, denial—especially in our own lives—can be quite subtle. At times, we can and often do present ourselves as blameless and project the problem onto someone or something else. The result may be negligible but sometimes the harm done is quite staggering.

Part of the cause of this problem is—once again!——our great fear of failure. We have an inflated sense of self which allows us to distance ourselves from others and compartmentalize our lives so we don't see our mistakes. It's as though we don't want our problems to come to light so we can learn about them and from them so we can be healed by God.

When we feel we have failed, there are possibilities to change. When we open ourselves to God totally, there are opportunities to be healed. But we must be open to the truth about ourselves. We must be open to the fact that our failure doesn't keep us from being loved by God.

Instead, the reality is: the denials, avoidances, and excuses we make become obstacles between ourselves and God. They serve to hide us from the very light we need to show us the way. And, it is senseless to hide from the warm loving light of God's love...even if, maybe especially if, we are feeling worthless or depressed. It is at these very moments that the opportunity to receive the grace to listen, understand, and change is specially present.

Sometimes we sit quietly for a moment and we experience a low period in our mood. We begin to question our life's purpose or quite simply the way we feel or have interpreted something. Then in the next fleeting moment, we feel foolish thinking this way and try to shake off what we perceive as momentary depression.

Yet, such moments can be helpful if we are not frightened, put off by them, or too quickly try to rationalize them based on our being tired, hungry, or overworked. They can be harbingers of hope if we don't try to run away. Feelings of apathy, minor sadness, boredom, or restlessness are sometimes the sounds of God traveling in our hearts to awaken us to the presence of a fragmented spirit.

Too often we run along trying to convince ourselves that everything is fine. What we are *doing* is great. Our sacrifices are appropriate. Our friends are numerous enough. And our family, parish, or community is getting ahead on schedule. But then this fleeting thought breaks through to ask us: "Are we in touch with God in our depths? Are we single-hearted enough? Are we remembering the single, dramatic call of Christ to remember. To remember what? To remember *to love*–to love strongly, to love always, to love the unlovable within ourselves, as well as the unlovable among those we meet and those we hear and read about (our distant 'family')."

Moments of alienation and depression can help us to raise our eyes to view a new horizon of hope instead of a darkness of spirit. They can awaken us to embrace our inner fragmentation and our outer interpersonal fences. They can shake us out of our complacency and righteousness and in a gentle spirit open us up to God.

And so, next time we feel low, maybe it is not a time to cry or run. Maybe it is a time to sit or kneel and wrap ourselves in gratitude to God. Gratitude for everything is needed—including the very act of stopping us or slowing us down so we can see how we have forgotten to love the presence of God in all creatures—including ourselves.

*Role of cognitive therapeutic principles
in assisting the process of discernment*

From a psychological angle of vision, this process of self-examination and listening to God can be made more possible and less self-deflating if we employ some of the psychological principles laid out by rational-emotive and cognitive therapists who focus on the connection between negative emotions (i.e., depression, anxiety) and distorted thinking and belief systems.

The cognitive principles established by Aaron Beck and his associates and further popularized by David Burns in his book *Feeling Good* are of particular relevance here. These investigators and clinicians have focused on how distorted thinking and illogical beliefs can lead to depressive emotions. By being aware of some of their tenets and the common faulty cognitive patterns they present, we can be helped to discern if our negative feelings are primarily due to a psychological cause. If we believe, with Karl Rahner, that theology is primarily a theological anthropology, then we will want to use everything at our disposal to understand the human condition. In this way, discerning between distorted thinking—which is primarily psychological—and spiritual impasse or desolation—which isn't—will be helpful.

In a case of mild depressive thinking, this may cut through the psychological difficulty sufficiently enough to surface the spiritual issues which need to be faced. To provide a sense of what I am referring to, the following several common distortions taken from Burns' book illustrate how people (and I would add especially perfectionistic Christians) fall prey to thinking errors that cause depressive feelings and an overall sense of discouragement:

> ALL OR NOTHING THINKING: You see things in black-and-white categories. If your performance falls short of perfect, you see yourself as a total failure...OVERGENERALIZATION: You see a single negative event as a never-ending pattern of defeat...MENTAL FILTER: You pick out a single negative detail and dwell on it exclusively so that your vision of all reality becomes darkened, like the drop of ink that discolors the entire beaker of water...DISQUALIFYING THE POSITIVE: You reject positive experiences by insisting that they

"don't count" for some reason or other. In this way you can maintain a negative belief that is contradicted by your everyday experiences...EMOTIONAL REASONING: You assume that your negative emotions necessarily reflect the way things are: "I feel it, therefore it must be true...SHOULD STATEMENTS: You try to motivate yourself with should and shouldn'ts...The emotional consequence is guilt. When you direct should statements toward others, you feel anger, frustration, and resentment...PERSONALIZATION: You see yourself as the cause of some negative external event which in fact you were not primarily responsible for.[12]

Negative thinking is quite common. For some reason, all of us seem to give more credence to the negative than to the positive. We can hear numerous positive things but somehow allow a few negative things to discolor and disqualify the previously affirming feedback we received. Therefore, we need to: (1) pick up and recognize our negative thinking so we can (2) link the negative thoughts we have to the depressive/anxious feeling we experience, so (3) the negative self-talk we have can be replaced with a more realistic thought or belief. It is in this way that we structure changing our negative thinking so our negative beliefs can eventually be modified as well.

We can always—and, unfortunately, frequently do—find a negative comparison to make when we are reflecting on our thoughts, actions, and motivations. Therefore, when we do reflect and discern, our faith stance (which says we are loved and special) must be held onto firmly. Unless we grasp and embrace this reality, we will be drawn into making harmful comparisons which will neither help us to learn about ourselves nor aid us to discern the Word of God in certain situations. Remember, finding something negative about ourselves is always easy. Making negative comparisons between our situations and those of others is never a problem. Maintaining perspective while we attempt to live simply in an anxious world is the difficulty!

We may say we already know this but can't seem to put it into practice. When I hear this statement I think of Mark Twain's comment: "The difference between the right word and the almost right word is the difference between lightning and the lightning bug." We may say we know it, but unless we can truly recognize and short-circuit the negativity that causes insecurity, increases defensiveness, and flies in the face of the reality that we are loved and have Christ within us, then we really don't know it. And it is this special knowledge that allows us to be open and take risks, as we must if we are to be true to our faith and ruthlessly honest in our discernment.

Rainer Maria Rilke, in his classic *Letters to a Young Poet*, wrote: "Only someone who is ready for everything, who excludes nothing, not even the most enigmatical, will live the relation to another as something alive and will himself draw exhaustively from his own existence. For if we think of this existence of the individual as a larger or smaller room, it appears evident that most people learn to know only one corner of their room, a place by the window, a strip of floor on which they will walk up and down. Thus they have a certain security. And yet that dangerous insecurity is so much more human which drives the prisoner in Poe's stories to feel out the shapes of their horrible dungeons and not be strangers to the unspeakable terror of their abode. We, however, are not prisoners. No traps or snares are set about us, and there is nothing which should intimidate or worry us....We have no reason to mistrust our world, for it is not against us. Has it terrors, they are *our* terrors; has it abysses, those abysses belong to us; are dangers at hand, we must try to love them."[13]

The point once again is: *how* we perceive something is more relevant than what we perceive. Our failures, as well as our successes, are beacons to light the way toward a self-understanding and self-love that will result in perspective, simplicity, service, and single-heartedness. But the beacon's light must have a source of energy that won't dissipate when it shines into the deep darkness of our personal illusions and anxieties. And the only source of energy that can last such a chilling psychological night and melt the inner narcissistic desire we have to escape with others who are also intent on denial, self-will, and personal idolatry is *faith.* It is the daily warm, serious, and will-full embrace of the gift of faith that makes appreciating our cognitive style (the way we think and believe) an opportunity to listen to God. Nothing else will substitute for faith; and if we try to find another replacement our hearts will know it.

Chapter Three
Seeing

I magery is one of the most under-examined *areas in psychotherapy and counseling. The power of employing imagery often doesn't occur to psychologists, psychiatrists, and other helping professionals. The process of mental health treatment is often very "left brain" in nature—that is, it is oriented to those functions primarily dealing with rational thinking. Consequently, opportunities for helping a person gain or regain perspective are lost.*

This lack of attention to imagery, unfortunately, is also evident in the processes of self-awareness and discernment with many people. Too often we look at what we thought in a certain situation without taking into consideration the information that comes from reviewing how we *viewed* both ourselves and others in certain interactions

Such an appreciation of imagery is essential, not only so we can pick up the images to see if they are appropriate, but also so we can place inspiring mental pictures before us, enabling us to respond in hope to the challenges God is calling us to meet. With a hope that is radically based on faith in the resurrection, we can develop imagery that will help us meet the challenges to risk as well as be enthusiastic, tenacious, and committed in our response to God. Moreover, with hope-infused images, our aim to be single-hearted can be supported because the other images that inspire a non-Christian lifestyle can be replaced. We must constantly be involved in an analysis of our own imagery so we can recognize the emotional pull of mental pictures which are not of the Christian philosophy that is at the heart of simplicity.

Risk

Sacred scriptures boldly challenge us—often in the person of Peter—to resist living a life that is safe and sound. Whether it is Christ meeting him at the gate running away, prompting Peter to ask: *"Quo vadis, Domine?"* ("Where are you going, Lord?") only to hear the stark reply: "I am going to Rome to be crucified again," or it is the movement of Peter out onto the waves (Mt 14:28–31), the message is clear: we must jump into the deep darkness of life if we expect to be in the presence of the light of God.

John Haughey's reflection on Matthew 14 emphasizes this theme. He says: "There seems to be another level of significance to this passage....It suggests that there are two ways of following the Risen Lord, one from the boat and another with him on the waves. There are, at least, two possible ways for a Christian to live his life. In the first way, he can enjoy the relative security of bark, numbers, and practice, although he might have to cope with the pervasive feeling that 'we are not really getting very far.' Or one can accompany Jesus on the waves and resign oneself to the precarious, almost capricious, it seems, element of the Spirit which, like the wind, 'blows wherever it pleases.' The second option puts one outside the social confirmation that one's milieu can provide. One's sole support is then much more starkly faith in the person of Christ Jesus. A life of complete faith propels one to live not by his own ideas, impulses, or abilities, but by the leadings of the Spirit that have much the same ebb and flow and unpredictability that wind and waves do."[1]

Yet, what choice do we have but to risk in hope? For, to quote Haughey again, "Each Christian is (somehow, in some way) the bearer of a Christology. He will be a letter written by the Spirit or he will be a carbon copy of what he has heard. If the latter, it will suggest that Jesus used to be and the Spirit never arrived."[2]

Enthusiasm and tenacity

Anthony Bloom has emphasized: "We must also remember that when we fulfill God's will...we must not do it tentatively, thinking of putting it to the test, to see what comes of it, because then it does not work....We must outgrow this attitude, be prepared to do God's will and pay the cost. Unless we are prepared to pay the cost, we are

wasting our time."[3] And in line with complete commitment he notes further that, "if we want to have a real encounter with God, we need more than mere organs of hearing and vision. We must have the enthusiasm, the desire, we must want to...see."[4]

Still, this enthusiasm is frequently absent. Many years ago in one of his conferences William McNamara focused directly on this when he asked: "Do we enter heaven by backing away from hell?" How we image God, ourselves, and others may well determine the answer to this question. If we see God as threatening rather than inspiring, we will be crushed by guilt; if we see ourselves as inadequate and lost rather than children of God, we will lose heart; and if we see others as against us rather than people who—despite some failings and misguided actions—are our brothers and sisters on the beachhead of the "kin-dom" of God, we will feel all alone...lost in an anxious world.

On the other hand, if our imagery—especially of God—is correctly Christian, a hope-filled life even amidst a troubled environment becomes possible. William Johnston points this out in terms of our symbolism. He indicates that "thousands of Christians'...mystical journey has begun with an obscure sense of presence, a conviction that God is close. He is around me and within me, without being identical with me. And as time goes on, I may reach the conviction (either gradually or in a flash) that I am loved and chosen and that I am called by name as was Moses."[5]

The rational stance we take is important. Notwithstanding this point though, it is often the image we have of God—the mental picture we have of our personal relationship with the Divine—that determines the strength of our desire to struggle to find and follow God. The following dialogue and the images it evokes emphasize this point dramatically:

> Each day the disciple would ask the same question: "How shall I find God?"
>
> And each day he would get the same mysterious answer: "Through desire."
>
> One day the Master happened to be bathing in the river with the disciple. He pushed the man's head under water and held it there while the poor fellow struggled desperately to break loose.
>
> Next day it was the Master who began the conversation: "Why did you struggle so when I held your head under water?"
>
> "Because I was gasping for air."
>
> "When you are given the grace to gasp for God the way you gasped for air, you will have found him."[6]

Simplicity and imagery

In addition to opening our hearts to receive imagery that greets grace, proper imagery can also help by guiding us away from the prevalent cultural norm to the counter-cultural Christian one we should follow. In *Celebration of Discipline*, Richard Foster writes: "The modern hero is the poor boy who becomes rich rather than the

Franciscan or Buddhist ideal of the rich boy who voluntarily becomes poor....Covetousness we call ambition. Hoarding we call prudence. Greed we call industry."[7] Whose view we hold then, how we see the world, will determine how we will behave. As Jesus states: "The eye is the lamp of your body. When your eyesight is sound, your whole body is lighted up, but when your eyesight is bad, your body is in darkness. Take care, then, that your light is not darkness. If your whole body is lighted up and not partly in darkness, it will be as fully illumined as when a lamp shines brightly for you" (Lk 11:34–36).

With hope, then, we are called to understand and employ imagery. Through its proper use we can pick up images that pull us down and replace them with ones that inspire us to meet God enthusiastically. With proper imagery we can find the good that is within us and within those we meet. And with a developing, maturing image of God, we can move to meet the living God instead of settling in with a god of our own fashion. Given this, what psychology can teach us with respect to imagery takes on a new import in our search for perspective and single-heartedness.

In the mind's eye

Personal mental imagery dramatically brightens or darkens the horizons for us. Yet, as was previously mentioned, despite its value, psychology and psychiatry have not made sufficiently good use of it. In counseling, or efforts at self-awareness/self-improvement, effective use of mental imagery can provide assistance in uncovering new information, in the development of self-esteem, and in preventing an erosion of one's self-confidence.

Arnold Lazarus, the founder of the Multi-Modal approach to treatment, is a strong proponent of the employment of the power of imagery for personal enrichment. In a book on the topic *(In the Mind's Eye)* he points out: "The use of imagery can often bypass verbal roadblocks and get to the root of the matter. Many people tend to over-intellectualize and they confuse everybody and themselves with verbiage....*Find* the images and you will understand the behavior." Further, find the images and, if you so desire, you will probably be able to *change* the feelings and the behavior."[8]

Living in an anxious world can lead to almost daily upset and confusion that is really unnecessary. One of the ways Lazarus suggests we try to uncover the reasons behind these feelings is to use associated imagery. He points out: "Obviously, when dealing with high degrees of anxiety, depression, and other emotional disturbances, a trained professional is essential. However, if you feel tense, or nervous, or otherwise upset, and you are unable to pinpoint why you are feeling bad, here is how you might use associated imagery:

1. Try to relax as much as possible.

2. Then return to the negative feelings and try to increase them. Thus, if you are feeling nervous, make yourself feel even more nervous; if angry, let your anger grow more intense.

3. Immediately focus on any image that comes to mind. Whatever that image happens to be, see it as vividly as possible. (Most people prefer doing imagery exercises with their eyes closed, but this is not essential.)

4. As you keep focusing on the image, others may take its place. If so, try to see each one as clearly as possible.

5. If different images do not come to mind, zero in on the original image as if using a zoom lens. Get really close up to it. This will assist you in associating different parts of the same image more meaningfully, or it will evoke other images for you to track.

6. As you follow each image, you may return to some of them, or to parts of these images. Just keep on seeing the images as clearly as you can.

This simple exercise often permits interesting insights and self-revelations to come to mind."[9]

Dr. Dorothy Suskind, who like Lazarus believes in the power of mental imagery, offers a slightly different approach. This time, rather than uncovering information, its goal is to use positive, success images to help people improve self-confidence and self-esteem so their behavior can reflect a positive mental outlook.[10]

The method referred to as the Idealized Self-Image (ISI) involves steps which include a relaxation exercise, imagery formation, recollection of past successes, and efforts at seeing the discrepancy between your real self (how you are now imaging yourself and what you are now doing) and your ISI (as you would like to be). However, although it is quite effective in increasing self-esteem, there is a danger of swinging to the other side of the problem—narcissism. In addition, there is also the possibility of getting so self-involved that the Christian community is diminished by our lack of meaningful involvement.

Consequently, I propose a modification of the

approach which for purposes of differentiation we may call the Idealized Christian Self-Image (ICSI). It avoids being caught in a distorted version of charismatic spirituality that is tied only to the resurrection (i.e., the present joy and power of the Spirit in the world and the self today) and balances it by also being tied to the cross (the necessary pain of Christian life) and ministry (the need to be involved with others) of Christ. The goal then is not merely to correct for one's inadequate self-image, so as to feel, think, and behave in a more personally rewarding way (although, this is an appropriate intermediate objective). Instead, it is also designed to help us be all that we can be and, in the process, to avoid unnecessary (neurotic) pain, so we can be open to serve fully as Christians.

The ICSI (Idealized Christian Self-Image) involves the following steps:

1. Sit down and reflect on what you would like your ICSI to be. In other words, select *specific* traits that are *within your abilities to achieve*. (For example, don't say "I wish to respond to God," because this is too broad. Instead, choose those traits that you believe support holiness—that is, commitment to taking out time for silence and solitude to pray reflectively, assertiveness in the face of injustice, involvement in the parish/prayer community.) Also, choose traits that are not only an extension of your present talents but also—to borrow a Jungian term—"dip into your shadow." By that I mean see yourself developing several parts of your personality that are very underdeveloped. So, if you are basically a good listener, picture yourself as speaking up and offering your opinion. This is not

so you will be replacing a basic interpersonal style (introverted type becoming totally extroverted) but is instead designed to bring out the fullness of your personality. Visually, it is like accenting the centerpiece of your personality with other hitherto ignored/denied aspects of it—much the same as you would place a rose in the middle of a vase and offset it with greens as a way of bringing out the flower's beauty.

2. Sit in a comfortable position and relax. Either do a relaxation exercise you may have learned or simply picture something peaceful and relaxing (i.e., seashore, mountains, a field of snow).

3. Bring your ICSI into focus and see how this differs from the present image you have of yourself. Doing this is essential for goal-setting so that you can monitor your progress in terms of behavior as well as the imagery, attitude, and feelings you have about yourself.

4. Picture people you know who possess these traits and image yourself acting like them. To reinforce this, recall specific successes in your life—for example, times when you acted like your ICSI in some way. Get in touch with the positive feelings you had when you succeeded in the past.

5. Adapt these feelings of accomplishments and success to the present. Image yourself in your present situation and what you are planning to do over the next week and month.

This approach should be used by taking out ten minutes in the beginning of the day to go through the above steps. However, of equal importance is to do the exercise informally during the day. When you are walking, speaking with someone, driving along, or attending a meeting, the image of the ICSI should be brought to mind as vividly as possible. And, if and when you see any conflict between the ICSI and your present action, steps should be taken to correct the discrepancy.

The result of this approach and its continued application is to create a positive, self-fulfilling prophecy that will be transmitted into behavior which will in turn reinforce the imagery. The following fictional case (that is modeled after actual ones) should bring this material to life.

Janet is a Roman Catholic professed woman religious in her early forties. She entered the convent in her mid-twenties, has an undergraduate degree in English, and a graduate degree in religious studies. She has been a teacher and director of religious education for the past thirteen years. She has enjoyed teaching, is well liked, personable, fairly quiet, and expresses some anxiety as to how people view her and whether she is being a "good religious" or not.

Recently, much to her surprise, she was asked not only to be the local minister of a convent where twelve sisters live, but also to serve on the diocesan staff as Coordinator of Religious Education. Although she accepted both posts, she was concerned about being the "superior" of twelve women who are all older—and probably more outspoken—than she. Also, she was a bit anxious about interacting with administrators, especially male clerics, in her new diocesan post.

In addition to assertiveness training and being helped to see the need to review her cognitive style (i.e., the way she would think about herself as a result of her interactions with others), she was asked to develop an ICSI. In response to this, she came up with the following attributes that she sees as reflective of her leadership and which were within her abilities if only she could "let go and be what she should be in the eyes of God." They were: to be calm, have a sense of "presence," be knowledgeable, and be free to speak up on what she believed in (even if this meant disagreement).

She was asked to reflect for ten minutes on her ICSI every morning prior to prayer and just after prayer. Also, she was asked to recall her ICSI as often as she could during the day. She did this for a week prior to moving into the convent where she would be the local minister. When she actually moved in, she found that she would view her quiet stance when people were talking to her not as shyness or anxiety but as quiet calm, poised presence—the "strong silent type." Then she noticed that, given this image, she began to speak up and ask questions so that she would become knowledgeable. Since her questions were the result of active listening—whereas in the past she would not hear what was being said because of anxiety as to what people would think—people reacted positively to her, and she did in fact become knowledgeable! And this in turn helped solidify her image of herself as an effective leader.

She was told to continue her ICSI and to add the incidences at the convent where she felt she was successful and reflect on them as often as possible when on the job at the diocesan office. These images then transferred into actions because she began to behave more in line with them. ("I thought to myself: Since I do have these gifts, why not use them? Even Jesus as a child reflected out loud on the Torah when he was with his elders in the temple because he felt he should share what knowledge he had. These other administrators may be more experienced, these men may be clerics, but we are all in baptism called to serve God.")

In some cases, she (in her words) "fell backward" when she received negative feedback or hostility when she spoke up. Following this, she was told to image the situation again, but much worse, and to image herself with poise and presence (a variation of Lazarus' "Step-Up" technique), not passivity or aggression, and to do this for a week. This completed the imagery work on this task since she began to fulfill the positive prophecy that was set out for her.

Imagery as an adjunct aid in spiritual/psychological development

Imagery techniques can also be employed as adjuncts to other psychological and spiritual methods used in the service of personal development. A good illustration of this today is the Enneagram. The Enneagram is based on Sufi wisdom that designates nine personality types. By discovering one's type and the compulsion that drives it, the belief is that it is possible to curb one's sinfulness and enhance one's giftedness.

The compulsion of one of those types, the "Three," is "to avoid failure. *Threes* grew up thinking their own personal worth consisted simply in the success of their achievements. As a consequence, they tend to put their whole identity as a person into the role they have. They may change roles in life but they value their whole life in terms of success and in the role they presently have. From the way they look at themselves, failure is intolerable. They put all their energy into succeeding in the task or role they have undertaken though ordinarily they undertake only what has a very good chance of succeeding and do not take on what could be risky."[11]

Imagery can help a person like this respond to God by moving them away from their compulsions while emphasizing their giftedness. By taking out time to image themselves as a child of God whose gifts are enthusiasm (rather than exhibitionism), achievement-oriented (rather than competitive), mission-oriented (rather than outcome-oriented), and loved by God from birth (rather than because of what they are doing now), freedom from the compulsion to succeed in the eyes of others and in their own eyes becomes more possible. The *Three* can then focus on what he/she believes God is calling him/her to do rather than on whether it is a "success" in the eyes of the world. Rather than being constantly on a stage giving exhausting performances, the *Three's* talents can be invested in responding with simplicity and single-mindedness to God.

Imagery then can help the *Three*, who is so concerned about image, performance, and personal failure, to embrace the words of Abbé Monchanin: "For us let it be enough to know ourselves to be in the place where God wants us, and carry on our work, even though it be no more than the work of an ant, infinitesimally small, and with unforeseeable results. Now is the hour of the garden and the night, the hour of the silent offering; therefore the hour of hope; God alone, faceless, unknown, unfelt, yet undeniably God."

Imagery offers us a true opportunity. As we harness the power of positive imagery we can join it with the vibrant imagery of sacred scriptures. We can image the human being as Christ did and image how we—given our own unique personality—can approach that image. Infused with a radical Christian hope that is based on a tenacious faith in the reality of the resurrection of Jesus, we can then move forward without anxiety and begin to behave—not out of compulsion or because we feel we should—but because we are in love.

Chapter Four

Service

Compassion is a hidden attitude of love. Our actions make visible this love or point to where our attitude, without our awareness, has somehow become distorted. So, explorations of our actions are important and beautifully complement the appreciation we seek of our cognition and imagery in our quest to respond simply and deeply to God.

What we *do* then can just as powerfully open up our hearts to the truth as a carefully experienced reflective period can. In some cases, as Parker Palmer notes, action may even take precedence in the discernment process. He relates: "On a visit to Koinonia Partners in Georgia, someone said words of revelation to us: 'You don't think your way into a new kind of living. You live your way into a new kind of thinking.'...Of course, my friend overstated the case. Our thinking and praying had prepared the soil to receive his words. But his counsel is a caution against the dangers of our linear, deductive approach to life: First think and pray, establish some principles and premises, then act upon them. That may be the way the life of facts operates, but not the life of the Spirit. The linear approach almost always becomes an infinite regress, always receding into finer and finer analyses while postponing the action that might reveal life anew to us....Action is revelatory. What we know about life is a function of where we stand in it, and by acting we take up a new standpoint."[1]

We are such a people of words. We talk about doing great things. We talk about improvement. We talk about failure. We even talk about prayer. Such talk alone brings us too far beyond the jetty of experience and we are caught in a sea of confusion where we have no navigation experience upon which to fall back. Is it any wonder that when a brother came to see Abba Theodore and started to talk and inquire about things which he himself had not tried yet, he received the advice: "Do your work first; then you will come to the point you are talking about now."[2]

God's surprise

The act of love then is a necessary part of our total response to God. Moreover, it allows God to surprise us in a way that we are carried onto the water as Peter was so we can greet the Lord on the waves.

When we are compassionate in our actions, the

attitude in place is essential. If we are acting out of love, then we will meet people quite openly. If there are other agendas in place which take primacy (to look good or to achieve results that *we* deem are important), the results can be disastrous. Therefore, it might be helpful to recall the following "paradigm of openness."

*　　*　　*

Paradigm of openness

• *Have low expectations and high hopes.* Have low expectations of people so you don't force them directly or indirectly to meet certain anticipations you might have as to how they should or should not respond to you and your actions. But have high hopes for them based on a ruthless faith in God that something good, something dear and beautiful will come of it if you are looking and listening with an open heart.

• *Forgive yourself and other people for their defensiveness.* Being cautious is natural for faithless and hopeless persons—and we all fall into this category more or less.

• *Be as open as possible to being surprised by the encounter.* In other words, we must not look for our god and reactions that we feel would be important and right. We must position ourselves instead to see whatever we will see amidst the joy, pain, apathy, anxiety, peace, depression, or tension we experience. When we are truly open, we will be surprised by something in the encounter. And that surprise—that unique presence of God—can be called by another name: *holiness.*

*　　*　　*

An illustration of this might be helpful here. Several years ago, a depressed patient whom I had seen for a number of years, came in to see me one afternoon for her weekly visit. She sat down and immediately said: "Last night I became aware that I was thankful to you; that you have brought Christ to me." To this I responded: "What prompted this thought?" She answered: "Well, I think many things must be going very well in your life and you are rewarded by them. Whether it's a course you're teaching, a book you're writing, or a patient you're seeing who has improved, all seems to be successful for you. Then there's *me*—a loser. It must be so hard sitting with me." To this I responded: "You are seeing things so negatively with respect to yourself. What makes you think you don't bring Christ to me?" In response (having had enough therapy to be assertive), she questioned my statement with the challenge: "How do I bring Christ to you?" I must admit if I hadn't been so open to the surprise of God, I would have had a hard time answering her; what I would have told her would have been an empty positive generalization. However, instead I was able to say: "If I can't see the Lord in your patience and persistence in dealing with this depression week after week, I don't know where I could possibly see him." Hearing this, she had to agree. My open eyes to the presence of God allowed me to share with her information that enabled her eyes to be opened as well.

Consequently, action without the right attitude and purpose can become mere motion. Too often behavior is not marked by an attitude of love but by anxiety, and unfortunately the goal is not the revelation of God's presence. Instead, it is a compulsive movement toward quelling our own self-esteem concerns. We are trying to imperson- ate rather than imitate Christ. As David Steindl-Rast rec- ognizes: "The do-gooder is too busy. He has no time to bother with flowers...the busybody does not understand the language of (the lilies') silent eloquence. He rushes on: 'Sorry, I don't speak lily.' His ears are buzzing with the din of his own projects, ideas, and good intentions."[3]

In such cases, our philosophy seems to be: If I work hard enough doing what I believe is right then I won't have to worry about what God is calling me to do, to be. In *operating* this way the "advantage" is that I can then replace the mystery of love, with the visible, manageable, measur- able quantity of "good works." Is it any wonder then that we spend so much energy trying to be dramatically success- ful Christians rather than simple-hearted ones?

Simple compassion

Too often in our search to do something dramatic we miss the opportunity to do something important because the act doesn't seem worthy enough. We are unable to see the symbolic greatness of the small caring presence we can be in a world seemingly overwhelmed by troubles and stress.

A brief illustration of nature may help in the visu- alization of this point. Bushes of roses brightening the roadside may be easily missed in the summertime. Yet, a single rose in the middle of a field of winter snow would never be overlooked. It stands out. The winter rose is a sign of hope, for its cheerful color seems to overshadow the competing drifts of cold and starkness. The same can be said of loving emotion and friendly gestures during times of anxiety, apathy, stress, and depression.

Kenneth Leech, in his book *True Prayer*, noted: "A facial expression or a warm hug is more than a symbol; it is a sacrament, for it expresses and conveys the personality behind it."[4] Mother Teresa also seems to recognize this in terms of relationships in general—especially in the fast-paced, efficient modern world in which we live. She tells the following story: "Some time ago a group of professors from the United States came to our house in Calcutta. Before leaving they said to me, 'Tell us something that will help us, that will help us become holy.' And I said to them, 'Smile at each other' (because we have no time even to look at each other)."[5]

In line with Mother Teresa's suggestion, maybe we are being called to try to take out the time to share a few moments, a few smiles, a few words with each other as the opportunities arise rather than being occasional dramatic Christians. Sometimes I wonder whether the good for which I am allowed to be a vehicle primarily occurs in the settings of my clinical work (i.e., office, hospital room) and teaching (i.e., classroom) or whether it takes place during those little daily chance encounters I have with persons with whom I live, work, and meet. Just as more learning seems to take place as a result of informal discussions between students in the hallways and in the cafeteria than in the classroom, the messages of love seem to be more readily received by others during the "off times," those times during the day when people don't have their defenses up and are open to casual interactions. Consequently, we need to be alert to the opportunities that abound for us to naturally—according to our own personality style—extend ourselves to others by not passing up the chances to listen, smile, laugh, and share a few helpful ideas.

Likewise, so our flame of love doesn't burn out, maybe we are also being called to appreciate others' symbolic behaviors of love. Thus, we should try to raise our level of attentive gratefulness so we can take advantage of the smiles, the verbal hugs and the concerned words that are already in our lives. Too often kindness, a passing word of support, or a smile is dismissed because the feeling is that it is not important ("That person smiles at everyone").

In the stressful world in which we live we have a responsibility now more than ever to catch ourselves when we are dismissing the importance of a gesture of caring—whether it is being given or received. The more we are able to catch the rays of interpersonal kindness that come our way, the more we can have our own human inner warmth fanned; the more we can reach out to everyone we meet with a sense of heart and hope (even if people don't seem to appreciate it in the way we would want them to), the more the cold emotions will be offset and overcome by warmth and caring.

We have a choice: we can see difficult times as a time to learn to appreciate that love is already in our lives and seek to share ourselves in "small" ways through caring conversation and thoughtful little gestures, or we can hide from the "now" and wait until the "springtime" to do "big" things for others. We have a choice: we can focus on the barren fields and cold streets of our own and others'

emotional "winters," or we can—with God's guidance—pick out the winter rose. It's up to us.

Henri Nouwen brings this point across in his use of the imagery of a clown. "Clowns are not the center of events. They appear between the great acts, fumble and fall, make us smile again after the tensions created by the heroes. They are people who, by their solitary lives of prayer and contemplation reveal to us our 'other side' and thus offer consolation, comfort, hope, and a smile. The large, busy, entertaining, and distracting world keeps tempting us to join the lion tamers and trapeze artist who get most of the attention. But whenever the clowns appear we are reminded that what really counts is something other than the spectacular and the sensational. It's what happens between the scenes. The clowns show us that our preoccupations, worries, tensions, and anxieties need a smile, but more important that we, too, have white on our faces and that we, too, are called to clown a little."[6]

Christians are called to be involved, to be *active.* Yet they are not called to be so *busy* that they become lost and overwhelmed in a maze of confusion. Consequently, to move from being a harried individual to being an effective, involved one, who is not torn apart, is an essential step to take if one is to remain alive and committed. To take such a step, there are a number of things that can be done:

1. *Never say you are busy!* Even if someone suggests that you are, reply that you are quite involved in a lot of activities but you don't feel busy. This will serve to stop reinforcement of the busy image; no longer will you get reinforced to be a martyr. (This step is harder than one

would think since while many of us complain about our schedule, we still enjoy the strokes we receive from others who see us as very busy: they feel sorry for us and give us the impression that we must be important since we are so busy. Therefore, we must be prepared for a good deal of resistance on our part to give up the "overworked, under-appreciated image.")

2. *Say "no" to people's request for your time if it is an inappropriate one.* If you are not sure or feel it is too hard to say "no," give an enthusiastic "maybe," and tell them you will get back to them tomorrow. This will give you twenty-four hours to decide what you want to do; if you decide against doing it, it will give you the time to structure your response and gain the stamina to set limits which may not be well received. (Sometimes exaggerating the anticipated negative response in your mind and imaging your handling it can deflate the anxiety that the actual situation produces.)

3. *Be present to the "now."* No matter how active you are, you can always deal with what each day presents if you don't preoccupy yourself with the rest of the demands facing you. What assists in this process is setting out planning times for the day and for longer periods (week, month, year). This is helpful when we are tempted to ruminate and mentally try (futilely of course) to gain control over our life. When we have a planning time we can quickly promise ourselves to look at whatever is at issue in the allotted time and to then return to the now. So, if we are driving and become preoccupied with things, we can quickly promise ourselves to think about them in the evening or the next morning (whenever the planning time

has been scheduled) so we can be released mentally to appreciate our present surroundings. Staying in the present isn't easy and will take a good deal of continual practice, but attentiveness to the now is important because it is not only spiritually sound, but it will also provides a good deal of psychological satisfaction and relief as well.

Being active for Christ is good. Being overwhelmed and too busy, because we don't have an asceticism of time and effort or an attitude that is fired by love instead of being driven by compulsiveness, obviously isn't. We not only have the responsibility to redeem our time, we have the ability to do it if we are willing to let go of our martyr image, set limits for others (given a willingness to recognize and accept our own limits), and be present to the moments of time and people that may be before us now. The choice is really not someone else's—despite our claim that our schedule is too full or others ask too much of us. The choice is actually ours—and we are asked to prayerfully make it each day. Ironically, not to prayerfully make such choices each day may well be more of an evasion of grace than not doing enough.

Hesitation to love

Romanticism fills our ideas about service but the reality is that reaching out with love can often be quite difficult and tedious. As Israel Baal Shem recognizes: "If a man falls into the mire and his friend wants to fetch him out, he must not hesitate to get himself a little dirty."[7]

This getting a "little dirty" often refers psychologically to the realization of how sensitive, suspicious, and prone to the defense of projection we are when in difficult or alien situations. Too often what makes us hesitate to help or, more commonly, continue to help is our personalization of, and hypersensitivity to, what people say and do to us. Our psyches are often like "negative flypaper" which picks up and interprets comments and actions in ways that are negative. We then use these against ourselves and/or project the blame for our negative thoughts and feelings onto others.

This is not a new observation. Merton, in his book on the desert fathers and mothers, focused on this point with respect to one of the most revered abbas. "It may come as a surprise to learn that St. Anthony, of all people, thought the devil had some good in him. This was not mere sentimentalism. It showed that in Anthony there was not much room left for paranoia. We can profitably reflect that modern mass-man is the one who has returned wholeheartedly to fanatical projections of all one's own evil upon 'the enemy' (whoever that may be). The solitaries of the desert were much wiser."[8]

Anthony de Mello also emphasizes the destructiveness of projection in the following dialogue:

> What is the greatest enemy of enlightenment?
> Fear.
> And where does fear come from?
> Delusion.
> And what is delusion?
> To think that the flowers around you are poisonous snakes.
> How shall I attain Enlightenment?
> Open your eyes and see.

What?
That there isn't a single snake around.[9]

So once again, while our behavior in the service of God is essential, it is the underlying attitude which determines how and with what intensity we will begin and continue our work. If we are willing to learn about ourselves as well as others, the work will continue. If we truly and tenaciously love ourselves as God loves us, the work will continue. If we are not seeking positive responses and great results but are trying to focus on finding God, the work will continue. But if our motivations are poor and our behavior lacks love (of *both* ourselves and those we serve), then the work will dry up and the seeds of despair, confusion, and bitterness may find root.

Motivation for service

Loving is easy if we are in touch with our own humanness, love ourselves, and in the process stop taking what we do so seriously as to be self-conscious. Too often service is an outgrowth of guilt. And maybe initially that isn't so bad. The prophets often tried to instill guilt in the peoples of the world so their hardened hearts could be broken up to the truth, so they would be able to care for each other again as God would have them care. Yet, guilt is not meant to be a sustaining force. Love is.

Guilt pushes us to do something because it is the right thing to do. Love encourages us to do something because it is the natural thing to do. The following brief story, *When Life Was Full There Was No History*, by Chuang Tzu illustrates this beautifully:

In the age when life on earth was full, no one paid any special attention to worthy men, nor did they single out the man of ability. Rulers were simply the highest branches on the tree, and the people were like deer in the woods. They were honest and righteous without realizing that they were 'doing their duty.' They loved each other and did not know that this was 'love of neighbor.' They deceived no one yet they did not know that they were 'men to be trusted.' They were reliable and did not know that this was 'good faith.' They lived freely together giving and taking, and did not know that they were generous. For this reason their deeds have not been narrated. They made no history.[10]

Love enables service then to be a natural, almost unconscious aspect of living. Compassionate behavior does not take into account the expectations of ourselves and others. Getting tied into expectations is often the beginning of the end of true service. When we feel we have done a good job or someone else rewards us for meeting his or her expectations, it obviously feels good. However, there must be a wariness about seeking to please so as to be rewarded.

Instead, the focus should be to love simply because loving is what we are called to do by God. We should give with a sense of *mitzvah* (giving and expecting nothing in return). By doing this we are setting the stage for God to act amidst our faith and the faith of the person(s) to whom we are being present. Rosemary Haughton recognizes this very process occurring during the time of Christ in a paper she entitles "Liberating the Divine Energy." An important point she makes is as follows: "One key was Jesus' sensitivity to actual individual people, in whom he perceived the operation of the same divine energy that was his own motive power. He knew them not only as acted upon by divine power but as sources of it....When he said to the paralytic, or the blind man or the shamed woman, '*Your faith has saved you—healed you*,' he was acknowledging the power of a transaction, a flowing of knowledge and power between them, in which his compassion was an essential agent yet one that was powerless without the response that somehow completed the circuit and transformed the situation."[11] The action of God must never be forgotten. Otherwise, discouragement will set in when the results expected by us and those with whom we interact don't materialize.

This theme is so beautifully presented by Thomas Merton in the following letter he wrote to a young activist, that I shall quote it almost in its entirety (italics supplied):

> Do not depend on the hope of results. When you are doing the sort of work you have taken on, essentially an apostolic work, you may have to face the fact that your work will be apparently worthless and even achieve no result at all, if not perhaps results opposite to what you expect. As you get used to this idea, you start more and more to concentrate not on the results but on the value, the truth of the work itself. And there, too, a great

deal has to be gone through, as gradually you struggle less and less for an idea and more and more for specific people. The range tends to narrow down, but it gets much more real. In the end, it is the reality of personal relationships that saves everything.

You are fed up with words, and I don't blame you. I am nauseated by them sometimes. I am also, to tell the truth, nauseated by ideals and with causes. This sounds like heresy but I think you will understand what I mean. It is so easy to get engrossed with ideas and slogans and myths that in the end one is left holding the bag, empty, with no trace of meaning left in it. And then the temptation is to yell louder than ever in order to make the meaning be there again by magic. Going through this kind of reaction helps you to guard against this. Your system is complaining of too much verbalizing, and it is right.

...the results are not in your hands or mine, but they suddenly happen, and we can share in them; but there is no point in building our lives on this personal satisfaction, which may be denied us and which after all is not that important.

The next step in the process is for you to see that your own thinking about what you are doing is crucially important. You are probably striving to build yourself an identity in your work, out of your work and your witness. You are using it, so to speak, to protect yourself against nothingness, annihilation. That is not the right use of your work. All the good that you will do will come not from you but from the fact that you have allowed yourself, in obedience of faith, to be used by God's love. Think of this more and gradually you will be free from the need to prove yourself, and you can be more open to the power that will work through you without your knowing it.

The great thing after all is to live, not to pour out your life in the service of a myth: and we turn the best things into myths. If you can get free from the domination of causes and just serve Christ's truth, you will be able to do more and will be less crushed by the inevitable disappointments. Because I see nothing whatever in sight but much disappointment, frustration and confusion...

The real hope, then, is not in something we think we can do, but *in God who is making something good out of it in some way we cannot see.* If we can do his will, we will be helping in this process. But we will not necessarily know all about it beforehand...

Enough of this...it is at least a gesture...I will keep you in my prayers.

All the best in Christ,

Tom[12]

At each of the phases of reaching out to others that Merton points to above, we may feel like charlatans, failures, and be tempted to become bitter or give up. Yet, these negative experiences can be the result of the presence of grace—a sign that God is not giving up on us and is still calling us to be obedient.

"Obedience" is a bad word to many people today. Yet, if we say that a flower is being obedient to the sun in trying to face it as best it can so as to encourage its own growth, we wouldn't see obedience as bad…just common sense and part of the natural order! Responding to God then by struggling to find his calling and following it is the only journey we need act upon; the results and the way people view us become incidental. Yet, once again, although this sounds straightforward enough, the journey is a dangerous one.

The dangerous journey

For a depressed person to get out of bed and interact with others is a true exercise in risk-taking. Still, we know from experience that this is just what he/she should do because activity tends to decrease depression. In a sense, we are asking the depressed person to *act on faith,* not what his/her thoughts are telling him/her to do (i.e., "You feel so terrible already; just stay in bed and away from people and you may feel better"). The belief as Teilhard de Chardin once noted is: "It doesn't matter if the water is cold or warm if you're going to have to wade through it anyway." And wade through it we must—even if we feel we are in over our heads!

Similarly, we are being asked in faith not to believe that our efforts are useless, even when the results seem elusive. We are being asked in faith not to believe that we are fools, even when more prudent people have given up trying to help. (How many people thought Mother Teresa was foolish to expect that her efforts would make an impact on the terrible conditions in Calcutta?) And we are being asked in faith not to see our feelings of futility, upset, stress, anxiety, or apathy as causes for despair, but as opportunities to learn that while we are tempted to meet our own expectations and those of others, this is not the purpose of helpful behavior.

The only purpose is, in love, to be of service to God: to be in the fullest sense of the message—to be a fool for Christ! This is the gamble we call "Christian living." And this gamble is often more than we can bear, as sometimes we feel the doubt, the question, the failure, the hostility, and (maybe even worse) the void. The reality we must face then is that if we live fully, it will on occasion be more than we can bear! That's why we need to be open to a deep relationship with God. And that's why in these anxious demanding times, we must take the most radical and useless step the eyes of the world have ever seen. We must pray.

Chapter Five
Experiencing

One of the important pieces of wisdom passed down to us from the desert fathers and mothers is that constant prayer can quickly straighten out our thoughts. Knowing this, and appreciating how thought also influences emotion, I think we can now safely say as well: "Constant prayer helps us to be quite in tune with the nuances of our affect." To prayerfully experience the movement of our moods enables us to be in touch with the pulse of our own deep feelings of closeness to, and distance from, the Lord.

James Fenhagen affirms this very theme in a unique way by noting: "Christian meditation leads us into personal encounter with the Lord. It opens up the deep places of our lives to the movement of the Spirit so that the Christ of the Gospel may permeate not only our rational processes, but those realms in which dreams and intuition are born."[1]

Yet, constant prayer—which paves the road to simplicity and single-heartedness—is frequently resisted by most of us, including those who proclaim their love for, and a special intentionality in their lives with respect to, God. In the words of Henri Nouwen: "We listen to lectures affirming the importance of prayer, but we really think that our people need actions and not prayer and that praying is good when you really have nothing else to do. I wonder if under the surface of our religiosity we do not have great doubts about God's effectiveness in our world, about his interest in us—yes, even about his presence among us. I wonder if many of us are not plagued by deep, hostile feelings toward God and the idea of God without having any way to express them. I even wonder if there are many religious people for whom God is their only concern....When we speak of our age as a secular age, we must first of all be willing to become aware of how deeply this secularism has entered into our own hearts and how doubt, hesitation, suspicion, anger, and even hatred corrode our relationship with God."[2]

Still, the desperate need for prayer obviously remains. And, ironically, the process of opening and continuing a deep dialogue with God not only puts us in greater touch with our thoughts, images, and feelings, but also transforms our attitude toward what we are *doing*. Again, in Nouwen's words: "Maybe we would be less pessimistic if we could live our limited actions as expressions of unlimited prayer. We may lose courage and confidence if we measure our value by counting those who are deeply affected by our actions, but when we remain aware of the countless people who can be embraced by our prayers, we can live joyfully and gratefully."[3]

Entering the uncharted zone

Prayer has gotten a bad name. It is often labeled as nice, harmless, warm, lovely, sweet, and soothing. These descriptions—and maybe even some other more accurate positive-oriented ones (i.e., "peaceful")—are somewhat misleading. For while the prayer life will surely bring with it at times a deep sense of well-being, this experience is neither the goal nor the necessary immediate result of a deep daily dialogue with God. Since any good intimate relationship is a precarious adventure at best, a committed relationship with God, guided by the process of prayer, is truly a dangerous as well as remarkable journey *if it is really undertaken in the spirit of the First Commandment*. If we were honest with ourselves about our relationship with God, I think we could all write a book entitled *God Is Solidly Number TWO in My Life!* We frequently put so many things and people (especially ourselves) in front of God. Therefore, we are rarely aware of the danger, the depth, the challenge, and the core of a real relationship with the Divine. We muse about it so much of the time rather than deciding to leave our world of rumination and procrastination and enter into a clear covenant with the Lord.

Only during those fleeting times when we really do venture out and actually do put prayer at the heart of our lives do we see what is at stake. The great Episcopal seminary dean, Urban Holmes, wrote several years before his death: "I recall once at a clergy conference asking the rhetorical question of those attending: 'How do you spend your time?' One man, to my surprise, answered: 'Helping people get through the night!' But pastors have no infra-red vision; it is just as dangerous for them to walk the path in the night as it is for persons they accompany—and a little more frightening, because they know how risky it is. Once and for all we need to lay aside every notion that the prayer life is easy or sure. The trail is marked with the spiritual graves of those who thought it was."[4]

What keeps us from true prayer?

Yet, having said all of this about the dangerous and elusive nature of a life prayerfully committed to God, the reality is that I think most of us are still willing to take the leap. In a world so filled with greed, anxiety, pressures, money-problems, confusion, and conflict, we do very much want the solace and challenge of the truth. We do want to gamble with our lives for the ultimate relationship. We do want to embrace the negative feelings of depression, anxiety, and stress that come into our lives and sit, stand, live, work, and play before God. We do dearly desire the growth-full opportunity to find perspective and unity within our questioning, torn heart and within the world that often tensely surrounds us. We do want our dull, subtly idolatrous world made new.

But the step toward God often seems so hard, so impossible, and foolishly (as is probably our habit) we blame God for this and fail to see our role in our experience of distance and alienation from the Divine. As Abraham Heschel notes: "We often lack the strength to be grateful, the courage to answer the ability to pray. To escape from the mean and penurious, from calculating and scheming, is at times the parching desire of man. Tired of discord, he longs to escape from his own mind—and for the peace of prayer. How good it is to wrap oneself in prayer, spinning a deep softness of gratitude to God around all thoughts, enveloping oneself in the silken veil of song! But how can man draw song out of his heart if his consciousness is a woeful turmoil of fear and ambition?"[5]

The answer to Heschel's question is obviously: to pray. Pray now, reflect during the day, pray always, and most of all pray *truly*; in other words, don't worry about what you say, how you say it, what you think about, and don't strain yourself, don't be concerned whether it is perfect or not—just love! As Heschel once again recognizes and describes beautifully: "To avoid prayer constantly is to force a gap between man and God which can widen into an abyss. But sometimes, awakening on the edge of despair to weep, and arising from forgetfulness, we feel how yearning moves in softly to become the lord of a restless breast, and we pass over the gap with the lightness of a dream."[6]

True prayer is always possible then. The question that needs to be answered is not whether—in my state—is opening up a dialogue with God possible; the question is: Am I in my self-involvement, insecurity, and denial ready to open myself up to the overwhelming generosity and challenges of being in a *real* relationship with God? And in the service of making a personal response possible am I willing to be aware of the need for:

1. being beautifully "ordinary" in a world so anxiously smitten with the desire to (deny death and God and) be seemingly extraordinary;

2. being open, truly open, to the wonder and awe that is in front of us right now and continually surrounds us everywhere;

3. seeking perspective amidst the joys and turmoil of everyday life.

How we are aware of these needs and seek to honestly respond to them may well determine if true prayer can grow, deepen, and expand within us to the point that when someone asks: "How is your 'prayer' life?" without knowing it they will really be asking: "How is your life?" Although we will have quiet time in solitude to spend in unique friendship with God, the relationship will always be there before us. The awe will not leave us even when our eyes are closed. That is the goal we must embrace; there is no desirable mid-ground.

Being ordinary

The call to be everyone but ourselves is so loud that we are usually not able to hear the "little voice of God" calling to us, to everything and everyone in nature to be fully

themselves. I find it hard to believe that human beings have the undesirable distinction in nature of being the only ones running away from the reality which has been given to them. Nothing else in nature does this. Isn't it ironic that, given the scale of plants, animals and humans of which we are on the top (I'm sure it is only coincidental that we made up the hierarchical scale and that we are on top of it!), we are the only species which spends so much time trying to be something or someone else. Tulips seek to be what they are—tulips. Dogs and bears simply respond to the call of nature to be as fully what they were created to be. Then there are we humans; what are we doing? We're trying to look and act in ways that would—to our eyes—make us more attractive. We are trying in so many ways to deny what realistically makes us—to our mind—ugly.

Consequently, in our prayers, in our sitting down and wrapping ourself in gratitude for all we are and all we have been given, one of the first preparations needed for true prayer to take place is: to be who we are before God. As Anthony Bloom points out: "Throughout the day we are a succession of social personalities, sometimes unrecognizable to others or even to ourselves. And when the time comes to pray and we want to present ourselves to God we often feel lost because we do not know which of these personalities is the true human person, and have no sense of our own true identity. The several successive persons that we present to God are not ourselves. There is something of us in each of them but the whole person is missing. And that is why a prayer which could rise powerfully from the heart of the true person cannot find its way between the successive men of straw we offer to God....How often our prayer is false because we try to present ourselves to God not as we are, but as we imagine he wants us to be. We come to him in our Sunday best or in borrowed finery. It is important that before we start to pray we should take time to recollect ourselves, to reflect and become aware of the real state in which we present ourselves to the Lord...this is the only real person there is in us. And God can save this person, however repellent he may be, because it is a true person. God cannot save the imaginary person that we try to present to him, or to others or ourselves. As well as seeking the real person in us, we must also seek constantly the person we are to God. We must seek for God in us and ourselves in God. This is the work of meditation which we should engage in every day all through our lives."[7]

Too often to our western minds, we see a miracle as something out of the ordinary, when, in reality, the truly ordinary, when it is seen in its purity, is actually a miraculous sight, because in the ordinary we can more "easily" see God's presence.

A number of years ago, a man was traveling in a rural area on the way to a city where he hoped he would close an important business deal. He was traveling very fast but had his car on cruise control, so the speed was automatically maintained on this long and quite deserted road, thus allowing him to enjoy the countryside a bit. Soon he became distracted by a splotch of color which was being reflected from somewhere down the road to the right.

He was intrigued by it and was amazed at the brilliance of the color. As he drove on he hoped his route would pass by it closely so he could see what it actually was.

After a few miles he was able to see that the color was coming from a building of some sort. Finally, as he drove even closer he saw that it appeared to be some kind of church. It was the middle of the day and he was amazed at the brilliance of the glass since the lights inside the church couldn't possibly account for the glass being seen so well during the day. He even mused that despite the out-of-the-way area in which the church was, the stained glass window must be one of the five or ten most brilliant in the world. After all, what else could account for it? He did love its color and radiance.

He became so intrigued and involved in his reverie about this window that when it came time at a fork in the road for him to drive away from the spot in the distance where he could see the window shining, he impulsively decided to take the road which would lead him closer to it.

With anticipation and excitement he drove toward it and could see it up on a rise in the land. As he drove around toward the front of the church though, he lost sight of it and the day became momentarily cloudy.

When he finally pulled around in front of the church, he saw that it wasn't really a church after all. It was just a shell of an old church. Only three walls stood. There were no doors and most of the windows were broken. Despite this scene, he quickly ran around to the front of the building to see the window he had admired from afar. When he got in front of this part of the church, he quickly looked up and his spirits immediately sank. For he was standing in front of a quite ordinary old window—not the window he dreamt about in his mind. The panes looked dusty; the frames were chipped; soon it would be blown out like the other windows.

He felt like such a fool. He shook his head and told himself how naive he had been. However, as he turned to leave, the cloud moved, and the brilliant sun shone through the window almost blinding him with its color. All of his skepticism left him; all of his disappointment was bathed clean with the warm colors he could feel covering him. Without his head being able to tell him what was going on, his heart felt it was in the presence of God.

This is what is possible with God when we are ordinary. We are like a stained glass window that is open to the "Son" shining through us. We are able to be true to being a way for others to experience God through us rather than being so involved in what image we feel we have to project. In prayer we are able, amidst all of our emotions—negative and positive alike—to find the deepest attitude, identity, and gift we have (what some people call "charism") and share it freely without the distraction of worrying whether we are being "successful" or coming across well. In such a state as this, we can also be open to the true wonder and awe that surrounds us and is in us.

Openness to true wonder and awe

Rabbi Samuel H. Dresner, an early student and long-time personal friend of Abraham Heschel, wrote of an important visit with Heschel: "Several years before Abraham Heschel's death in 1972, he suffered a near fatal heart attack from which he never fully recovered. I traveled to his apartment in New York to see him. He had gotten out of bed for the first time to greet me, and was sitting in the living room when I arrived, looking weak and pale. He spoke slowly and with some effort, almost in a whisper. I strained to hear his words....'Sam,' he said, 'when I regained consciousness, my first feelings were not of despair or anger. I felt only gratitude to God for my life, for every moment I had lived. I was ready to depart. 'Take me, O Lord,' I thought. 'I have seen so many miracles in my lifetime.'...Exhausted by the effort, he paused for a moment, then added: 'This is what I meant when I wrote...'I did not ask for success; I asked for wonder. And you gave it to me.'"[8] If only all of us could say this to our God.

The wonder and awe that the world we and others fabricate is paltry compared to God's offerings. We need only look at the colors of nature in the fall or the fury of a storm in the winter to see what God can communicate to us even when we can only "half-see" through the distractions of being preoccupied with the hurts of the past and a desire to control the future, while the vibrant present before us remains almost totally ignored and unappreciated.

This is why silence and a sense of presence to the now are so encouraged by so many spiritual writers. Silence breaks down the walls and attention to the now helps one to see what has long been hidden behind them.

The value of silence has long been appreciated. This is nothing new. Kallistos Ware reflects a commonly held belief when he says: "In an age when language has been disgracefully trivialized, it is vital to rediscover the power of the word; and this means rediscovering the nature of silence, not just as a pause between words but as one of the primary realities of existence."[9] One of the tenets of *The Jerusalem Community Rule of Life* adds to this by directly admonishing: "Live your silence, don't merely endure it. You will love it only if you learn its value and its cost."[10]

The valuable silence to which the rule refers is obviously not a mere absence of noise, but a stance of patience and openness. A person of true prayer who is able to live a deep silence then is (in Thomas Merton's words) "not the one who prepares his mind for a particular message that he wants or expects to hear, but who remains empty because he knows that he can never expect or anticipate the word that will transform his darkness into light. He does not even anticipate a special kind of transformation. He does not demand light instead of darkness. He waits on the Word of God in silence, and when he is 'answered,' it is not so much by a word that bursts into his silence. It is by his silence itself suddenly, inexplicably revealing itself to him as a word of great power, full of the voice of God."[11]

Confucius also said many, many years ago: "Look at this window: it is nothing but a hole in the wall, but because of it the whole room is full of light. Being full of light it becomes an influence by which others are secretly transformed."[12] This window of which he speaks is, for me, silence—the true silence that allows God to speak.

Yet, given all of this we often resist solitude, silence, and an opening up of ourselves. Possibly we do this, not only because we are unfamiliar and uncomfortable with the absence of noise and busyness in our lives, but also because of the things which "come up" when all is quiet. As William Johnston notes: "When one enters the desert (whether real or metaphorical) without books and magazines, without radio and T.V., when one's senses are no longer bombarded by all the junk to which we are ordinarily exposed, when the top layers of our psyche are swept clean and bare and empty—then the deeper layers of the psyche rise to the surface. The inner demons lift up their ugly faces. The snakes and scorpions which were dormant or hard at work in the unconscious now raise their venomous heads and slithered into the conscious mind. And we are face to face with the evil."[13]

What does Johnston mean by all of this? Well, Parker Palmer illustrates this to some degree when he reflects on his initial encounters with the silence of Society of Friends' (Quaker) meetings: "I had come to the silence with a headful of religious ideas and beliefs. In the silence, they all fell away, structures without foundations. In the silence I was forced to confront the ambiguities of my own religious experience, and I grew angry about what I found there, about the discrepancies between my inherited faith and my own faithless life."[14]

And so, silence (and the solitude that sometimes needs to accompany it in order to make the experience of quiet deep enough) sets the stage to dramatically open up a number of doors—doors which will not only let the spiritual fresh air of new insight, experiences and consolation in, but also open up the possibility of letting the deep resistances to God come to the surface. This is reflected in a particular way in another dialogue presented by de Mello:

"'Where can I find God?' 'He's right in front of you.' 'Then why do I fail to see him?' 'Why does the drunkard fail to see home?' Later the Master said, 'Find out what it is that makes you drunk. To see you must be sober.'"[15]

In the spirit of John of the Cross and the desert fathers and mothers, William McNamara, a contemporary contemplative who enjoys the gifts of life but tries not to make them an end in themselves, warns that we must, in our silence and solitude, not only become aware of our idols but vigorously act to remove them. A number of years ago, he emphasized this theme in the following way: "The contemplative is easily pleased and deeply nourished precisely because he comes to the other empty-handed. It is hard for God or Beethoven to put anything into a closed fist. A cluttered mind or a crowded heart impedes the art of contemplation and therefore precludes any pleasurable consequences. That is why St. John of the Cross is so pitilessly hard on appetites. They fritter away our capacity for ecstasy. Every time we pander to these frivolous intruders, possibilities of real pleasures dwindle. Just when the waiter comes with champagne, our glasses are full of Kool-Aid."[16] And so, letting go does not mean just emptying ourselves and risking facing the darkness, it also means opening ourselves up in joy and responsiveness to the glory of "flowing with God."

When one of the desert fathers, for example, approached the saintly sage Abba Joseph to question about the natural movement of the spiritual life, he received a response that would certainly transform his life, and any who could really listen to him relate what happened. "Abba Lot went to see Abba Joseph and said: 'Abba, as much as I am able I practice a small rule, a little fasting, some prayer and meditation, and remain quiet, and as much as possible I keep my thoughts clean. What else should I do?' Then the old man stood up and stretched out his hands toward heaven, and his fingers became like ten torches of flame. And he said: "If you wish, you can become all flame.'"[17] This is what we are all called to as sisters and brothers of Christ; and this is what we all resist in our movement away from God and our loss of perspective.

Seeking perspective in prayer

Prayer radically pulls us down from an existence in our illusions and lifts us back up into the reality for which we were created. Instead of being concerned with controlling life or avoiding the specter of our own image and mortality, it faces us with our limits and helps us to live fully within them.

As William Johnston notes, Ignatius of Loyola "would constantly reflect on the inner movements, examine our consciousness and detect not only any inner movements toward sin but also the movements which lead to anxiety, fear, commotion, loss of peace. For in one who would travel the path to God, as the great goods are peace and joy and the other fruits of the spirit, so the greatest evils after sin are turmoil and anxiety leading to loss of faith, loss of hope, loss of charity, and change of commitment."[18]

Consequently, while prayer may at times seem hard, unproductive, dry, or haphazard, and even though it might call us to do things that are not easy, in all instances prayer seeks *freedom* for us: freedom from unnecessary anxiety, depression, turmoil, stress, apathy, anger, loneliness, and anomie. Prayer says to us that life is both hard and wonderful enough without seeking either needless pain or artificial thrills. It advises us that while we shouldn't avoid the stress that comes with following the Lord, we must be careful not to indiscriminately carry crosses which are not meant for us.

Prayerful perspective can come out of our meeting our emotions with honesty, interest, and a desire to learn. In our quiet moments of reflection, we can sense the pulse of our feelings but this is not enough. What we feel must lead us to what we think and believe about ourselves, our Lord, and our universe. It must also lead us back again and again to the sacred scriptures and must call us to our knees again and again to realize the place of grace.

Karl Barth once indicated that if we critically read the Bible the way we should, it will in turn confront us. As we try to uncover what it is trying to say to us, it will ask of us: Who are we who are reading it? Our discernment concerning the Word will simultaneously involve a rediscovery of our identity in Christ.

If this doesn't take place, it could well be that we are not attacking each word as if life were held in it. Merton once wrote: "Curiously the most serious religious people, or the most concerned scholars, those who constantly read the Bible as a matter of professional or pious duty, can often manage to evade a radically involved dialogue with the book they are questioning....Let us not be too sure we know the Bible just because we have learned not to be astonished at it, just because we have learned not to have problems with it. Have we perhaps learned at the same time not to really pay attention to it? Have we ceased to fight it? Then perhaps our reading is no longer serious."[19]

Being serious with the Bible isn't easy. It is a very frightening book. What it asks as well as what it promises is almost too much to face. Yet we must admit that we are over our heads—we can't face the demands without God's grace-full support; we can't totally absorb Jesus' words "you are my friends" (Jn 15:14).

What we can do is to stop avoiding the opportunities to truly read the scriptures, to sit in silence, and to patiently and courageously face our emotions so we can learn about ourselves and our movements toward and away from God. If we are patient, if we are open, we will learn—we will feel the presence of God.

For years I would read the scriptures and quietly pray that I could be more obedient to God, more single-hearted. For years I would pray that I could be enthusiastic rather than exhibitionistic, achievement-oriented rather than competitive. For years, being an impetuous person, I would pray that I would not be swayed by people's reactions—positive or negative—or be a victim of my insecurities and need to be liked, but only be concerned with doing God's will. And for years the sense I received in prayer was simply: "Just do my will; it is enough." And to this I would always reply in a very down-to-earth way: "It's easy for you to say! I just can't do it. It's not enough for me. I need a reward. If it's not people's good thoughts, if it's not the applause, if it's not my image, then I must have something."

Then one day, when I was praying for something else, I sensed a response not only to this request, but also finally to my original one as well. The impression I had was this: "You have asked that you not be concerned with your image or success but only with my will; your prayer will be answered now." To this I became anxious and was even sorry I had prayed for help at all. I was concerned that with the gift more would be asked of me. (My lack of faith and sinfulness continues to astound and almost overwhelm me.) Yet, this insecurity did not dispel the sense I had of God's presence. And the impression I had of the Lord's response continued clearly in the following manner: "If you seek to do my will and focus only on it and not on your success or the way people respond, you will find you won't have to worry about whether or not you are accepted and loved by others. You shall have another reward that will make you secure—in *every* lecture, in *every* therapy hour, in *every* encounter on the street, when you only concern yourself with doing my will and forget about the reactions or results, you will be *in the Presence of the Spirit*....Is that enough?"

No response on my part was obviously needed. No response, I guess, is ever needed to a promise Jesus made long ago—one which I was only able (with the grace of God) to hear clearly now: "I will not leave you orphaned; I will come back to you" (Jn 14:18).

There is an ancient Buddhist saying: "When you are ready, the teacher will appear." Yes, I think this is so. And I believe that I have experienced this. But I think you can't be ready if you are not silent, present, alert, and aware of a fact we so easily forget: the results are, in the last analysis, *not* in our hands. While we are mandated to use all of our talents to discern how God is calling us to seek perspective and be single-hearted, we must also patiently embrace the reality of our total dependence on grace (a lesson beautifully taught by those from the Reformed tradition). Not to recognize this final point is to fall prey to the disillusionment that can come when "deadly clarity fades."[20] And it is at this point that even the most personally and spiritually mature can become seriously lost on the journey and risk skepticism or even despair.

Chapter Six
Deadly Clarity

From a psychological perspective, sin is primarily the result of denying, ignoring, or worshiping our personality instead of nurturing it in light of the Gospel call to respond in faith, hope, and love. When, due to false humility, anxiety, or a lack of trust and hope, we deny that Christ is present in us, we fail to rejoice in the gifts God has given us to share with others. When we ignore the possibilities of God in our personality, we bury our talents and prevent their natural growth and "outgrowth" to others. And when we worship our personality as compensation for feelings of insecurity or recognition of our mortality and limitedness, we move God over and become the center and goal of our universe—we deny our discipleship.

Instead, we are invited to perspective. In the spirit of original sin we are called to discern any innate/learned "loyalty to the negative." Consequently, when we feel depressed, anxious, insecure, upset, distressed, or unloved, we must seek out our distorted thinking, inaccurate imagery, and evidences of compulsive behavior that are driven by a desire to meet our own and others' unrealistic expectations instead of the ones God is simply setting before us. In the spirit of original blessing, we must open ourselves up to the gifts God continually places before us. Not to do so is not merely foolish, it is dangerous. It keeps us from being fully alive in a world that needs Divine energy reflected in the attitudes and actions of the people of God.

Yet, having emphasized the extreme importance of expending all due effort to achieve as much clarity as possible in seeking and serving God, the search for clarity itself is fraught with a particular danger that must be taken into consideration: namely, psychology and rational knowledge are not synonyms for "deep spirituality"; the place of grace must never be forgotten or underestimated. If we do forget or underestimate grace, God will surely remind us of its significance.

God is a mystery. Karl Rahner, the great theologian, recognized this when, on the occasion of his eightieth birthday, he gave a presentation which "might be interpreted as his spiritual testament. He implored theologians to stay mindful of the absolute mystery of God as the single decisive theme of theology."[1] This theme is very much in line with his theology of the child, which I think can be our theme as adults as well: "The child is conscious that it has nothing of itself, that everything has to be received as gift. It lives waiting for the unexpected, trusting the unpredictable...."[2]

Mystery and impasse are the "stuff" of which certain periods of the spiritual life are made. And just as we make the greatest use of our knowledge, we must also know when to bow to our lack of rational power. Constance FitzGerald puts this beautifully in her paper "Impasse and the Dark Night": "A genuine impasse situation is such that the more action one applies to escape it, the worse it gets....Thorough-going impasse forces one, therefore, to end one's habitual methods of acting by a radical breaking out of the conceptual blocks that normally limit one's thinking....The psychologists and the theologians, the poets and the mystics, assure us that impasse can be the condition for creative growth and transformation if the experience of impasse is fully appropriated within one's heart and flesh with consciousness and consent; if the limitations of one's humanity and human condition are squarely faced and the sorrow of finitude allowed to invade the human spirit with real, existential powerlessness; if the ego does not demand understanding in the name of control and predictability but is willing to admit the mystery of its own being and surrender itself to this mystery; if the path into the unknown, into the uncontrolled and unpredictable margins of life, is freely taken when the path of deadly clarity fades."[3]

Sometimes then, the call is not to reason things out, because we have done our best and the situation still seems full of confusion, darkness, and an absence of progress. The call is to be like pilots flying at very high altitudes. When they fly at such heights it is hard to determine by looking at the horizon which side is "up" and which is "down." If they go by their eyes, they may fly upside down—they must go by their instruments and "forget" what they see. In impasse, in darkness, our eyes may see failure, alienation, despair, and injustice, but we must continue in patience and perseverance guided by the only instrument that can help us to continue to move forward even though our heart seems to tell us otherwise: *faith.*

If anything, impasse and helplessness even in the face of all we know or try to recognize can dramatically drive us to recognize and embrace the reality of grace. The danger is always present that we will see knowledge as a master rather than a servant or our talents as certain means rather than tentative steps to finding our way on the journey toward God.

Security is an illusion when we rely only on ourselves and can lead us astray just as quickly as when we leave everything in God's hands and avoid taking our place and being available to God, so Divine compassion can be shown through us in some way. As Elaine Prevallet notes in her insightful pamphlet *Reflections on Simplicity,* in order to be single-minded we must first see what divides us. "Simplicity means having a clear focus on the one thing necessary, an undivided heart. Jesus says it this way: no one can serve two masters (Mt 6:24). He doesn't say you ought not, or you may not, but you *can* not. It isn't possible. With his customary incisiveness, Jesus isn't talking about how it should be, the ideal world; he is enunciating the deepest laws of life. He's saying this is how it *is*. You can't, in fact, worship more than one God. Jesus also says that where our treasure is, there our hearts will also be (Mt 6:21). What do we want more than anything in the world? For most of us, the truthful answer is our own security. If security is our treasure, then we need to look there to find our idols, for we can't belong wholly to God as our one master, or dedicate ourselves to the service of others if in fact our hearts are mastered by another treasure. To put it a different way, we can't become single-hearted or single-minded unless we confront our double-heartedness and double-mindedness....What makes us double-minded? Trying to find security in more than one thing. The more objects, persons, situations outside myself I look to for security, the more multiple-minded I am; or if there are a thousand things I need to make me secure, then I am thousand-minded. Human security is a delicate thing."[4]

Anxiety, feeling "down" or bored, stress, and upset are often indications that we have put our hands psychologically around something/someone less than God: our hearts are divided. Sometimes that "something" is our intelligence and rationality, and these negative emotions are not punishments but are gentle or firm reminders of the fact that we have deluded ourselves. They are calls to vigorously pursue perspective while "actively waiting" in patience for God to intervene. An upside-down iron flute without holes or mouthpiece is an image for the Zen metaphor for the vain attempt to solve the secret of life with logic.[5] Yet how often do we pick up the iron flute of knowledge and blow on it until we pass out because we are oblivious of the place of grace, of God, in our lives!

The tension is always there (what is in our hands—what is in God's?) but so is the reward. The reason I say this is that even in impasse we can hope, and even in defeat of our best efforts we can be enthusiastic, *if* only we don't shy away from the only really God-given question we must face in an anxious world: How can I truly love (God, myself, others) *now?*

We must recognize that the answer to this question may be only good for the moment. The Spirit moves where she will. Finding out how I must love *now* is the thrill of life; and settling now for the answer I came up with in my response to God yesterday is to try to be secure in a way that will always leave us with the queasy feeling: "I'm missing something." There is never a substitute for searching actively and continually looking in wonder and awe for perspective. We must be willing and patient, in spite of our talents and the call to develop them, to be dependent on the Divine. Being on the edge of mystery with God is what life is all about. And if we don't panic when this mystery seems much too much like a depressing, hopeless shroud over our possibilities, the light will dawn. After all, this is what Jesus promised, didn't he?

Notes

Chapter One. An Introduction to Perspective

    1. Anthony de Mello, *One Minute Wisdom*, New York: Doubleday, 1986, p. 32.

    2. Robert Wicks, *Availability: The Problem and the Gift*, Mahwah, N.J.: Paulist Press, 1986, p. 15.

    3. Albert Nolan, *Spiritual Growth and Option for the Poor*, Speech given to the Catholic Institute for International Relations, London, at its annual meeting, June 29, 1984.

    4. David Steindl-Rast, *Gratefulness, The Heart of Prayer*, Mahwah, N.J.: Paulist Press, 1984, p. 142.

    5. *Ibid.*, p. 145.

    6. Jose L. Gonzales-Balado and Janet Playfoot (eds.), *My Life for the Poor: The Story of Mother Teresa in Her Own Words*, San Francisco: Harper and Row, 1985, p. 76.

    7. James Fenhagen, *Invitation to Holiness*, San Francisco: Harper and Row, 1985, p. 57.

    8. Peter Schaefer, *Amadeus* (screenplay).

Chapter Two. Listening

1. Robert Wicks, "Clarity and Obscurity: Critical Thinking Cognitive Psychotherapeutic Principles in the Service of Spiritual Discernment," *Thought* 63, no. 248 (May 1988): 77–85.

2. Anthony de Mello, *One Minute Wisdom,* New York: Doubleday, 1986, p. 64.

3. Thomas Merton, *The Silent Life,* New York: Farrar, Straus, and Giroux, 1957, p. 13.

4. James Fenhagen, *More Than Wanderers: Spiritual Disciplines for Christian Ministry,* Minneapolis: Seabury, 1978, pp. 7–8.

5. Thomas Merton, *Spiritual Direction and Meditation,* Collegeville, Minn.: Liturgical Press, 1960, p. 99.

6. *The Jerusalem Community Rule of Life,* Mahwah, N.J.: Paulist Press, 1985, p. 68.

7. William Sloane Coffin, *Once to Every Man,* quoted in William Hulme, *Managing Stress in Ministry,* San Francisco: Harper and Row, 1985, pp. 54–55.

8. Thomas Merton, *The Way of Chuang Tzu,* New York: New Directions, 1965, p. 102.

9. Yushi Nomura, *Desert Wisdom,* New York: Doubleday, 1982, p. 45.

10. William Johnston, *Christian Mysticism Today,* San Francisco: Harper and Row, 1984, pp. 74–76.

11. Donald Senior, "Prayer According to John," *Praying,* no. 10 (Winter 1986).

12. David Burns, *Feeling Good,* New York: New American Library, 1980, pp. 40–41.

13. Rainer Maria Rilke, *Letters to a Young Poet,*

revised edition (translated by M. D. Herter Norton), New York: Norton, 1954, pp. 68-69.

Chapter Three. Seeing

    1. John Haughey, *Conspiracy of God: The Holy Spirit in Men*, Garden City: Doubleday, 1973, pp. 61-62.

    2. *Ibid.*, pp. 31-32.

    3. Anthony Bloom, "Meditation and Worship," in: *Modern Spirituality*, edited by John Garvey, Springfield, Ill.: Templegate, 1985, pp. 34-35.

    4. Anthony Bloom, *Courage To Pray*, Mahwah, N.J.: Paulist Press, 1973, p. 12.

    5. William Johnston, *Christian Mysticism Today*, San Francisco: Harper and Row, 1984, p. 27.

    6. Anthony de Mello, *One Minute Wisdom*, New York: Doubleday, 1986, p. 43.

    7. Richard Foster, *Celebration of Discipline*, San Francisco: Doubleday, 1978, pp. 70-71.

    8. Arnold Lazarus, *In the Mind's Eye*, New York: Guilford, 1984, p. 36.

    9. *Ibid.*, pp. 17, 18.

    10. Dorothy Suskind, "The Idealized Self-Image (ISI)," *Behavior Therapy* 1 (1970): 538-41.

    11. Maria Beesing, Robert J. Nogosek, and Patrick H. O'Leary, *The Enneagram: A Journey of Self-Discovery*, Denville, N.J.: Dimension, 1984.

Chapter Four. Service

    1. Parker Palmer, "The Spiritual Life: Apocalypse Now," in: *Living with Apocalypse: Spiritual Resources*

for Social Compassion, edited by Tilden Edwards, San Francisco: Harper and Row, 1984, pp. 30–31.

2. Yushi Nomura, *Desert Wisdom*, New York: Doubleday, 1982, pp. 28–29.

3. David Steindl-Rast, *Gratefulness, The Heart of Prayer*, Mahwah, N.J.: Paulist Press, 1984, p. 156.

4. Kenneth Leech, *True Prayer: An Invitation to Christian Spirituality*, San Francisco: Harper and Row, 1980, p. 4.

5. Jose L. Gonzales-Balado and Janet Playfoot (eds.), *My Life for the Poor: The Story of Mother Teresa in Her Own Words*, San Francisco: Harper and Row, 1985, p. 82.

6. Henri Nouwen, *Clowning in Rome*, New York: Doubleday, 1979, pp. 2–3.

7. Martin Buber, *Tales of the Hasidim: Early Masters*, New York: Schocken Books, 1947, p. 7.

8. Thomas Merton, *Wisdom of the Desert*, New York: New Directions, 1960, pp. 21–22.

9. Anthony de Mello, *One Minute Wisdom*, New York: Doubleday, 1986, p. 78.

10. Thomas Merton, *The Way of Chuang Tzu*, New York: New Directions, 1965, p. 76.

11. Rosemary Haughton, "Liberating the Divine Energy," in *Living with the Apocalypse*, edited by Tilden Edwards, San Francisco: Harper and Row, 1984, p. 78.

12. James H. Forest, "Thomas Merton's Struggle with Peacemaking," in *Thomas Merton: Prophet in the Belly of a Paradox*, edited by Gerald Twomey, Mahwah, N.J.: Paulist Press, 1978, pp. 52–53.

Chapter Five. Experiencing

1. James Fenhagen, *More Than Wanderers: Spiritual Discipline for Christian Ministry*, Minneapolis: Seabury, 1978, p. 8.

2. Henri Nouwen, *Clowning in Rome*, New York: Doubleday, 1979, p. 26.

3. *Ibid.*, p. 32.

4. Urban Holmes, *Spirituality for Ministry*, San Francisco: Harper and Row, 1984, p. 37.

5. Abraham Heschel, "The Sigh," in *Modern Spirituality: An Anthology*, edited by John Garvey, Springfield, Ill.: Templegate, 1985, p. 10.

6. *Ibid.*, p. 14.

7. Anthony Bloom, *Courage To Pray*, Mahwah, N.J.: Paulist Press, 1973, pp. 18-20.

8. Samuel Dresner (editor), *I Asked for Wonder: A Spiritual Anthology of Abraham Heschel*, New York: Crossroad, 1986, p. vii.

9. Kalistos Ware, "The Spiritual Father in: Orthodox Christianity," in *Modern Spirituality: An Anthology*, edited by John Garvey, Springfield, Ill.: Templegate, 1985, pp. 45-46.

10. *The Jerusalem Community Rule of Life*, Mahwah, N.J.: Paulist Press, 1985, p. 23.

11. Thomas Merton, *Contemplative Prayer*, New York: Doubleday, 1969, p. 90.

12. Thomas Merton, *The Way of Chuang Tzu*, New York: New Directions, 1965, p. 53.

13. William Johnston, *Christian Mysticism Today*, San Francisco: Harper and Row, 1984, p. 55.

14. Parker Palmer, "The Spiritual Life: Apocalypse Now," in *Living with the Apocalypse*, edited by Tilden Edwards, San Francisco: Harper and Row, 1984, p. 37.

15. Anthony de Mello, *One Minute Wisdom*, New York: Doubleday, 1986, p. 52.

16. William McNamara, *The Human Adventure*, Garden City: Doubleday, 1974, p. 80.

17. Yushi Nomura, *Desert Wisdom*, New York: Doubleday, 1982, p. 90.

18. William Johnston, *op. cit.*, p. 69.

19. Thomas Merton, *Opening the Bible*, Collegeville, Minn.: Liturgical Press, 1970, p. 27.

20. Constance FitzGerald, "Impasse and the Dark Night," in *Living with the Apocalypse*, edited by Tilden Edwards, San Francisco: Harper and Row, 1984, p. 96.

Chapter Six. Deadly Clarity

1. Karl Rahner, *Words of Faith*, edited by Robert Scherer, New York: Crossroad, 1987, p. ix.

2. *Ibid.*, p. ix.

3. Constance FitzGerald, "Impasse and the Dark Night," in *Living with the Apocalypse*, edited by Tilden Edwards, San Francisco: Harper and Row 1984, pp. 96-97.

4. Elaine M. Prevallet, *Reflection on Simplicity*, Pendle-Hill, Pa.: Pendle-Hill, 1982, pp. 9-10.

5. Peter Matthiessen, *Nine-Headed Dragon River: Zen Journals 1969-1982*, Boston: Shambala, 1986, p. 39.

ILLUMINATIONBOOKS

Other Books in the Series

Little Pieces of Light...Darkness and Personal Growth
    by Joyce Rupp

Lessons from the Monastery That Touch Your Life
    by M. Basil Pennington, O.C.S.O.

As You and the Abused Person Journey Together
    by Sharon E. Cheston

Spirituality, Stress & You
    by Thomas E. Rodgerson

Joy, The Dancing Spirit of Love Surrounding You
    by Beverly Elaine Eanes

Every Decision You Make Is a Spiritual One
    by Anthony J. De Conciliis with John F. Kinsella

Celebrating the Woman You Are
    by S. Suzanne Mayer, I.H.M.

Why Are You Worrying?
    by Joseph W. Ciarrocchi

Partners in the Divine Dance of Our Three Person'd God
    by Shaun McCarty, S.T.

Love God...Clean House...Help Others
    by Duane F. Reinert, O.F.M. Cap.

Along Your Desert Journey
    by Robert M. Hamma

Appreciating God's Creation Through Scripture
    by Alice L. Laffey

Let Yourself Be Loved
    by Phillip Bennett

Facing Discouragement
    by Kathleen R. Fischer and Thomas N. Hart